The Ric…

Bab…ylon

Original 1926 Edition

By George S. Clason

Reprint edition by Dauphin Publications Inc, 2023, www.daupub.com

ISBN 9781939438850

TABLE OF CONTENTS

ABOUT THE AUTHOR: George was born in Louisiana on Nov. 7, 1874. He attended the University of Nebraska and served in the U.S. Army during the Spanish-American War. Beginning a long career in publishing, he founded the Clason Map Company of Denver, CO, and published the first road atlas of the U.S. and Canada. In 1926, he issued the first of a famous series of pamphlets on thrift and financial success, using parables set in ancient Babylon to make each of his points. These were distributed in large quantities by banks and insurance companies and became familiar to millions, the most famous being *The Richest Man in Babylon*, the parable from which the present volume takes its title. These "Babylonian parables" have become a modern inspirational classic.

dauphin publications

Foreword

Our prosperity as a nation depends upon the personal financial prosperity of each of us as individuals.

This book deals with the personal successes of each of us. Success means accomplishments as the result of our own efforts and abilities. Proper preparation is the key to our success. Our acts can be no wiser than our thoughts. Our thinking can be no wiser than our understanding.

This book of cures for lean purses has been termed a guide to financial understanding. That, indeed, is its purpose: to offer those who are ambitious for financial success an insight which will aid them to acquire money, to keep money and to make their surpluses earn more money.

In the pages which follow, we are taken back to Babylon, the cradle in which was nurtured the basic principles of finance now recognized and used the world over.

To new readers the author is happy to extend the wish that its pages may contain for them the same inspiration for growing bank accounts, greater financial successes and the solution of difficult personal financial problems so enthusiastically reported by readers from coast to coast.

To the business executives who have distributed these tales in such generous quantities to friends, relatives, employees and associates, the author takes this opportunity to express his gratitude. No endorsement could be higher than that of practical men who appreciate its teachings because they, themselves, have worked up to important successes by applying the very principles it advocates.

Babylon became the wealthiest city of the ancient world because its citizens were the richest people of their time. They appreciated the value of money. They practiced sound financial principles in acquiring money, keeping money and making their money earn more money. They provided for themselves what we all desire. . . incomes for the future.

George. S. Clason

1. The Man Who Desired Gold

Bansir, the chariot builder of Babylon, was thoroughly discouraged. From his seat upon the low wall surrounding his property, he gazed sadly at his simple home and the open workshop in which stood a partially completed chariot.

His wife frequently appeared at the open door. Her furtive glances in his direction reminded him that the meal bag was almost empty and he should be at work finishing the chariot, hammering and hewing, polishing and painting, stretching taut the leather over the wheel rims, preparing it for delivery so he could collect from his wealthy customer.

Nevertheless, his fat, muscular body sat stolidly upon the wall. His slow mind was struggling patiently with a problem for which he could find no answer. The hot, tropical sun, so typical of this valley of the Euphrates, beat down upon him mercilessly. Beads of perspiration formed upon his brow and trickled down unnoticed to lose themselves in the hairy jungle on his chest.

Beyond his home towered the high terraced wall surrounding the king's palace. Nearby, cleaving the blue heavens, was the painted tower of the Temple of Bel. In the shadow of such grandeur was his simple home and many others far less neat and well cared for. Babylon was like this—a mixture of grandeur and squalor, of dazzling wealth and direst poverty, crowded together without plan or system within the protecting walls of the city.

Behind him, had he cared to turn and look, the noisy chariots of the rich jostled and crowded aside the sandaled tradesmen as well as the barefooted beggars. Even the rich were forced to turn into the gutters to clear the way for the long lines of slave water carriers, on the "king's business," each bearing a heavy goatskin of water to be poured upon the hanging gardens.

Bansir was too engrossed in his own problem to hear or heed the confused hubbub of the busy city. It was the unexpected twanging of the strings from a familiar lyre that aroused him from his reverie. He turned and looked into the sensitive, smiling face of his best friend—Kobbi, the musician.

"May the gods bless thee with great liberality, my good friend," began Kobbi with an elaborate salute. "Yet, it does appear they have already been so generous thou needest not to labor. I rejoice with thee in thy good fortune. More, I would even share it with thee. Pray, from thy purse which must be bulging else thou wouldst be busy in your shop, extract but two humble shekels and lend them to me until after the noblemen's feast this night. Thou wilt not miss them ere they are returned."

"If I did have two shekels," Bansir responded gloomily, "to no one could I lend them—not even to you, my best of friends; for they would be my fortune—my entire fortune. No one lends his entire fortune, not even to his best friend."

"What," exclaimed Kobbi with genuine surprise, "Thou hast not one shekel in thy purse, yet sit like a statue upon a wall! Why not complete that chariot? How else canst thou provide for thy noble appetite? Tis not like thee, my friend. Where is thy endless energy? Doth something distress thee? Have the gods brought to thee troubles?"

"A torment from the gods it must be," Bansir agreed. "It began with a dream, a senseless dream, in which I thought I was a man of means. From my belt hung a handsome purse, heavy with coins. There were shekels which I cast with careless freedom to the beggars; there were pieces of silver with which I did buy finery for my wife and whatever I did desire for myself; there were pieces of gold which made me feel assured of the future and unafraid to spend the silver. A glorious feeling of contentment was within me! You would not have known me for thy hardworking friend. Nor wouldst have known my wife, so free from wrinkles was her face and shining with happiness. She was again the smiling maiden of our early married days."

"A pleasant dream, indeed," commented Kobbi, "but why should such pleasant feelings as it aroused turn thee into a glum statue upon the wall?"

"Why, indeed! Because when I awoke and remembered how empty was my purse, a feeling of rebellion swept over me. Let us talk it over together, for, as the sailors do say, we ride in the same boat, we two. As youngsters, we went together to the priests to learn wisdom. As young men, we shared each other's pleasures. As grown men, we have always been close friends. We have been contented subjects of our kind. We have been satisfied to work long hours and spend our earnings freely. We have earned much coin in the years that have passed, yet to know the joys that come from wealth, we must dream about them. Bah! Are we more than dumb sheep? We live in the richest city in all the world. The travelers do say none equals it in wealth. About us is much display of wealth, but of it we ourselves have naught. After half a lifetime of hard labor, thou, my best of friends, hast an empty purse and sayest to me, "May I borrow such a trifle as two shekels until after the noblemen's feast this night?" Then, what do I reply? Do I say, "Here is my purse; its contents will I gladly share?' No, I admit that my purse is as empty as thine. What is the matter? Why cannot we acquire silver and gold—more than enough for food and robes?

"Consider, also, our sons," Bansir continued, "are they not following in the footsteps of their fathers? Need they and their families and their sons and their sons' families live all their lives in the midst of such treasurers of gold, and yet, like us, be content to banquet upon sour goat's milk and porridge?"

"Never, in all the years of our friendship, didst thou talk like this before, Bansir." Kobbi was puzzled.

"Never in all those years did I think like this before. From early dawn until darkness stopped me, I have labored to build the finest chariots any man could make, soft-heartedly hoping someday the gods would recognize my worthy deeds and bestow upon me great prosperity. This they have never done. At last, I realize this they will never do. Therefore, my heart is sad. I wish to be a man of means. I wish to own lands and cattle, to have fine robes and coins in my purse. I am willing to work for these things with all the strength in my back, with all the skill in my hands, with all the cunning in my mind, but I wish my labors to be fairly rewarded. What is the matter with us? Again I ask you! Why cannot we have our just share of the good things so plentiful for those who have the gold with which to buy them?"

"Would I know an answer!" Kobbi replied. "No better than thou am I satisfied. My earnings from my lyre are quickly gone. Often must I plan and scheme that my family be not hungry. Also, within my breast is a deep longing for a lyre large enough that it may truly sing the strains of music that do surge through my mind. With such an instrument could I make music finer than even the king has heard before."

"Such a lyre thou shouldst have. No man in all Babylon could make it sing more sweetly; could make it sing so sweetly, not only the king but the gods themselves would be delighted. But how mayest thou secure it while we both of us are as poor as the king's slaves? Listen to the bell! Here they come." He pointed to the long column of half-naked, sweating water bearers plodding laboriously up the narrow street from the river. Five abreast they marched, each bent under a heavy goatskin of water.

"A fine figure of a man, he who doth lead them." Kobbi indicated the wearer of the bell who marched in front without a load. "A prominent man in his own country, 'tis easy to see."

"There are many good figures in the line," Bansir agreed, "as good men as we. Tall, blond men from the north, laughing black men from the south, little brown men from the nearer countries. All marching together from the river to the gardens, back and forth, day after day, year after year. Naught of happiness to look forward to. Beds of straw upon which to sleep—hard grain porridge to eat. Pity the poor brutes, Kobbi!"

"Pity them I do. Yet, thou dost make me see how little better off are we, free men though we call ourselves."

That is truth, Kobbi, unpleasant thought though it be. We do not wish to go on year after year living slavish lives. Working, working, working! Getting nowhere."

"Might we not find out how others acquire gold and do as they do?" Kobbi inquired.

"Perhaps there is some secret we might learn if we but sought from those who knew," replied Bansir thoughtfully.

"This very day," suggested Kobbi, "I did pass our old friend, Arkad, riding in his golden chariot. This I will say, he did not look over my humble head as many in his station might consider his right. Instead, he did wave his hand that all onlookers might see him pay greetings and bestow his smile of friendship upon Kobbi, the musician."

"He is claimed to be the richest man in all Babylon," Bansir mused.

"So rich the king is said to seek his golden aid in affairs of the treasury," Kobbi replied.

"So rich," Bansir interrupted, "I fear if I should meet him in the darkness of the night, I should lay my hands upon his fat wallet."

"Nonsense," reproved Kobbi, "a man's wealth is not in the purse he carries. A fat purse quickly empties if there be no golden stream to refill it. Arkad has an income that constantly keeps his purse full, no matter how liberally he spends."

"Income, that is the thing," ejaculated Bansir. "I wish an income that will keep flowing into my purse whether I sit upon the wall or travel to far lands. Arkad must know how a man can make an income for himself. Dost suppose it is something he could make clear to a mind as slow as mine?"

"Me thinks he did teach his knowledge to his son, Nomasir," Kobbi responded. "Did he not go to Nineveh and, so it is told at the inn, become, without aid from his father, one of the richest men in that city?"

"Kobbi, thou bringest to me a rare thought." A new light gleamed in Bansir's eyes. "It costs nothing to ask wise advice from a good friend and Arkad was always that. Never mind though our purses be as empty as the falcon's nest of a year ago. Let that not detain us. We are weary of being without gold in the midst of plenty. We wish to become men of means. Come, let us go to Arkad and ask how we, also, may acquire incomes for ourselves."

Thou speakest with true inspiration, Bansir. Thou bringeth to my mind a new understanding. Thou makest me to realize the reason why we have never found any measure of wealth. We never sought it. Thou hast labored patiently to build the staunchest chariots in Babylon. To that purpose was devoted your best endeavors. Therefore, at it thou didst succeed. I strove to become a skillful lyre player. And, at it I did succeed.

"In those things toward which we exerted our best endeavors we succeeded. The gods were content to let us continue thus. Now, at last, we see a light, bright like that from the rising sun. It biddeth us to learn more that we may prosper more. With a new understanding we shall find honorable ways to accomplish our desires."

"Let us go to Arkad this very day," Bansir urged, "Also, let us ask other friends of our boyhood days, who have fared no better than ourselves, to join us that they, too, may share in his wisdom."

"Thou wert ever thus thoughtful of thy friends, Bansir. Therefore hast thou many friends. It shall be as thou sayest. We go this day and take them with us."

2. The Richest Man in Babylon

In old Babylon there once lived a certain very rich man named Arkad. Far and wide he was famed for his great wealth. Also was be famed for his liberality. He was generous in his charities. He was generous with his family. He was liberal in his own expenses. But nevertheless each year his wealth increased more rapidly than he spent it.

And there were certain friends of younger days who came to him and said: "You, Arkad, are more fortunate than we. You have become the richest man in all Babylon while we struggle for existence. You can wear the finest garments and you can enjoy the rarest foods, while we must be content if we can clothe our families in raiment that is presentable and feed them as best we can.

"Yet, once we were equal. We studied under the same master. We played in the same games. And in neither the studies nor the games did you outshine us. And in the years since, you have been no more an honorable citizen than we.

"Nor have you worked harder or more faithfully, insofar as we can judge. Why, then, should a fickle fate single you out to enjoy all the good things of life and ignore us who are equally deserving?"

Thereupon Arkad remonstrated with them, saying, "If you have not acquired more than a bare existence in the years since we were youths, it is because you either have failed to learn the laws that govern the building of wealth, or else you do not observe them.

" 'Fickle Fate' is a vicious goddess who brings no permanent good to anyone. On the contrary, she brings ruin to almost every man upon whom she showers unearned gold. She makes wanton spenders, who soon dissipate all they receive and are left beset by overwhelming appetites and desires they have not the ability to gratify. Yet others whom she favors become misers and hoard their wealth, fearing to spend what they have, knowing they do not possess the ability to replace it. They further are beset by fear of robbers and doom themselves to lives of emptiness and secret misery.

"Others there probably are, who can take unearned gold and add to it and continue to be happy and contented citizens. But so few are they, I know of them but by hearsay. Think you of the men who have inherited sudden wealth, and see if these things are not so."

His friends admitted that of the men they knew who had inherited wealth these words were true, and they besought him to explain to them how he had become possessed of so much prosperity, so he continued:

"In my youth I looked about me and saw all the good things there were to bring happiness and contentment. And I realized that wealth increased the potency of all these.

"Wealth is a power. With wealth many things are possible.

"One may ornament the home with the richest of furnishings. "One may sail the distant seas.

"One may feast on the delicacies of far lands.

"One may buy the ornaments of the gold worker and the stone polisher.

"One may even build mighty temples for the Gods.

"One may do all these things and many others in which there is delight for the senses and gratification for the soul.

"And, when I realized all this, I decided to myself that I would claim my share of the good things of life. I would not be one of those who stand afar off, enviously watching others enjoy. I would not be content to clothe myself in the cheapest raiment that looked respectable. I would not be satisfied with the lot of a poor man. On the contrary, I would make myself a guest at this banquet of good things.

"Being, as you know, the son of a humble merchant, one of a large family with no hope of an inheritance, and not being endowed, as you have so frankly said, with superior powers or wisdom, I decided that if I was to achieve what I desired, time and study would be required.

"As for time, all men have it in abundance. You, each of you, have let slip by sufficient time to have made yourselves wealthy. Yet, you admit, you have nothing to show except your good families, of which you can be justly proud.

"As for study, did not our wise teacher teach us that learning was of two kinds: the one kind being the things we learned and knew, and the other being the training that taught us how to find out what we did not know?

"Therefore did I decide to find out how one might accumulate wealth, and when I had found out, to make this my task and do it well. For, is it not wise that we should enjoy while we dwell in the brightness of the sunshine, for sorrows enough shall descend upon us when we depart for the darkness of the world of spirit?

"I found employment as a scribe in the hall of records, and long hours each day I labored upon the clay tablets. Week after week, and month after month, I labored, yet for my earnings I had naught to show. Food and clothing and penance to the Gods, and other things of which I could remember not what, absorbed all my earnings. But my determination did not leave me.

“And one day Algamish, the money lender, came to the house of the city master and ordered a copy of the Ninth Law, and he said to me, ‘I must have this in two days, and if the task is done by that time, two coppers will I give to thee.’

“So I labored hard, but the law was long, and when Algamish returned the task was unfinished. He was angry, and had I been his slave, he would have beaten me. But knowing the city master would not permit him to injure me, I was unafraid, so I said to him, ‘Algamish, you are a very rich man. Tell me how I may also become rich, and all night I will carve upon the clay, and when the sun rises it shall be completed.’

“He smiled at me and replied, ‘You are a forward knave, but we will call it a bargain.’

“All that night I carved, though my back pained and the smell of the wick made my head ache until my eyes could hardly see. But when he returned at sunup, the tablets were complete.

“ ‘Now,’ I said, ‘tell me what you promised.’

“ ‘You have fulfilled your part of our bargain, my son,’ he said to me kindly, ‘and I am ready to fulfill mine. I will tell you these things you wish to know because I am becoming an old man, and an old tongue loves to wag. And when youth comes to age for advice he receives the wisdom of years. But too often does youth think that age knows only the wisdom of days that are gone, and therefore profits not. But remember this, the sun that shines today is the sun that shone when thy father was born, and will still be shining when thy last grandchild shall pass into the darkness.

“ ‘The thoughts of youth,’ he continued, ‘are bright lights that shine forth like the meteors that oft make brilliant the sky, but the wisdom of age is like the fixed stars that shine so unchanged that the sailor may depend upon them to steer his course.

“ ‘Mark you well my words, for if you do not, you will fail to grasp the truth that I will tell you, and you will think that your night’s work has been in vain.’

“Then he looked at me shrewdly from under his shaggy brows and said in a low, forceful tone, ‘I found the road to wealth when I decided that *a part of all I earned was mine to keep*. And so will you.’

“Then he continued to look at me with a glance that I could feel pierce me but said no more.

“ ‘Is that all?’ I asked.

“ ‘That was sufficient to change the heart of a sheep herder into the heart of a money lender,' he replied.

" 'But *all* I earn is mine to keep, is it not?' I demanded.

" 'Far from it,' he replied. 'Do you not pay the garment-maker? Do you not pay the sandal-maker? Do you not pay for the things you eat? Can you live in Babylon without spending? What have you to show for your earnings of the past month? What for the past year? Fool! You pay to everyone but yourself. Dullard, you labor for others. As well be a slave and work for what your master gives you to eat and wear. If you did keep for yourself one-tenth of all you earn, how much would you have in ten years?'

"My knowledge of the numbers did not forsake me, and I answered, 'As much as I earn in one year.'

" 'You speak but half the truth,' he retorted. 'Every gold piece you save is a slave to work for you. Every copper it earns is its child that also can earn for you. If you would become wealthy, then what you save must earn, and its children must earn, that all may help to give to you the abundance you crave.

" 'You think I cheat you for your long night's work,' he continued, 'but I am paying you a thousand times over if you have the intelligence to grasp the truth I offer you.

" 'A part of all you earn is yours to keep. It should be not less than a tenth no matter how little you earn. It can be as much more as you can afford. Pay yourself first. Do not buy from the clothes-maker and the sandal-maker more than you can pay out of the rest and still have enough for food and charity and penance to the Gods.

" 'Wealth, like a tree, grows from a tiny seed. The first copper you save is the seed from which your tree of wealth shall grow. The sooner you plant that seed the sooner shall the tree grow. And the more faithfully you nourish and water that tree with consistent savings, the sooner may you bask in contentment beneath its shade.'

"So saying, he took his tablets and went away.

"I thought much about what he had said to me, and it seemed reasonable. So I decided that I would try it. Each time I was paid I took one from each ten pieces of copper and hid it away. And strange as it may seem, I was no shorter of funds, than before. I noticed little difference as I managed to get along without it. But often I was tempted, as my hoard began to grow, to spend it for some of the good things the merchants displayed, brought by camels and ships from the land of the Phoenicians. But I wisely refrained.

"A twelfth month after Algamish had gone he again returned and said to me, 'Son, have you paid to yourself not less than one-tenth of all you have earned for the past year?'

"I answered proudly, 'Yes, master, I have.'

" 'That is good,' he answered beaming upon me, 'and what have you done with it?'

" 'I have given it to Azmur, the brickmaker, who told me he was traveling over the far seas and in Tyre he would buy for me the rare jewels of the Phoenicians. When he returns we shall sell these at high prices and divide the earnings.'

" 'Every fool must learn,' he growled, 'but why trust the knowledge of a brickmaker about jewels? Would you go to the breadmaker to inquire about the stars? No, by my tunic, you would go to the astrologer, if you had power to think. Your savings are gone, youth, you have jerked your wealth-tree up by the roots. But plant another. Try again. And next time if you would have advice about jewels, go to the jewel merchant. If you would know the truth about sheep, go to the herdsman. Advice is one thing that is freely given away, but watch that you take only what is worth having. He who takes advice about his savings from one who is inexperienced in such matters, shall pay with his savings for proving the falsity of their opinions.' Saying this, he went away.

"And it was as he said. For the Phoenicians are scoundrels and sold to Azmur worthless bits of glass that looked like gems. But as Algamish had bid me, I again saved each tenth copper, for I now had formed the habit and it was no longer difficult.

"Again, twelve months later, Algamish came to the room of the scribes and addressed me. 'What progress have you made since last I saw you?'

" 'I have paid myself faithfully,' I replied, 'and my savings I have entrusted to Aggar the shield maker, to buy bronze, and each fourth month he does pay me the rental.'

" 'That is good. And what do you do with the rental?'

" 'I do have a great feast with honey and fine wine and spiced cake. Also I have bought me a scarlet tunic. And some day I shall buy me a young ass upon which to ride.'

"To which Algamish laughed, 'You do eat the children of your savings. Then how do you expect them to work for you? And how can they have children that will also work for you? First get thee an army of golden slaves and then many a rich banquet may you enjoy without regret.' So saying he again went away.

"Nor did I again see him for two years, when he once more returned and his face was full of deep lines and his eyes drooped, for he was becoming a very old man. And he said to me, 'Arkad, hast thou yet achieved the wealth thou dreamed of?'

"And I answered, 'Not yet all that I desire, but some I have and it earns more, and its earnings earn more.'

" 'And do you still take the advice of brickmakers?'

" 'About brickmaking they give good advice,' I retorted.

" 'Arkad,' he continued, 'you have learned your lessons well. You first learned to live upon less than you could earn. Next you learned to seek advice from those who were competent through their own experiences to give it. And, lastly, you have learned to make gold work for you.

" 'You have taught yourself how to acquire money, how to keep it, and how to use it. Therefore, you are competent for a responsible position. I am becoming an old man. My sons think only of spending and give no thought to earning. My interests are great and I fear too much for me to look after. If you will go to Nippur and look after my lands there, I shall make you my partner and you shall share in my estate.'

"So I went to Nippur and took charge of his holdings, which were large. And because I was full of ambition and because I had mastered the three laws of successfully handling wealth, I was enabled to increase greatly the value of his properties. So I prospered much, and when the spirit of Algamish departed for the sphere of darkness, I did share in his estate as he had arranged under the law."

So spake Arkad, and when he had finished his tale, one of his friends said, "You were indeed fortunate that Algamish made of you an heir."

"Fortunate only in that I had the desire to prosper before I first met him. For four years did I not prove my definiteness of purpose by keeping one-tenth of all earned? Would you call a fisherman lucky who for years so studied the habits of the fish that with each changing wind he could cast his nets about them? Opportunity is a haughty goddess who wastes no time with those who are unprepared."

"You had strong willpower to keep on after you lost your first year's savings. You are unusual in that way," spoke up another.

"Willpower!" retorted Arkad. "What nonsense. Do you think willpower gives a man the strength to lift a burden the camel cannot carry, or to draw a load the oxen cannot budge? Willpower is but the unflinching purpose to carry a task you set for yourself to fulfillment. If I set for myself a task, be it ever so trifling, I shall see it through. How else shall I have confidence in myself to do important things? Should I say to myself, 'For a hundred days as I walk across the bridge into the city, I will pick from the road a pebble and cast it into the stream,' I would do it. If on the seventh day I passed by without remembering, I would not say to myself, 'Tomorrow I will cast two pebbles which will do as well.' Instead, I would retrace my steps and cast the pebble. Nor on the twentieth day would I say to myself, 'Arkad, this is useless. What does it avail you to cast a pebble every day? Throw in a handful and be done with it.' No, I would not say that nor do it. When I set a task for myself, I complete it. Therefore, I am careful not to start difficult and impractical tasks, because I love leisure."

And then another friend spoke up and said, "If what you tell is true, and it does seem as you have said, reasonable, then being so simple, if all men did it, there would not be enough wealth to go around."

"Wealth grows wherever men exert energy," Arkad replied. "If a rich man builds him a new palace, is the gold he pays out gone? No, the brick maker has part of it and the laborer has part of it, and the artist has part of it. And everyone who labors upon the house has part of it. Yet when the palace is completed, is it not worth all it cost? And is the ground upon which it stands not worth more because it is there? And is the ground that adjoins it not worth more because it is there? Wealth grows in magic ways. No man can prophesy the limit of it. Have not the Phoenicians built great cities on barren coasts with the wealth that comes from their ships of commerce on the seas?"

"What then do you advise us to do that we also may become rich?" asked still another of his friends. "The years have passed and we are no longer young men and we have nothing put by."

"I advise that you take the wisdom of Algamish and say to yourselves, *'A part of all I earn is mine to keep.'* Say it in the morning when you first arise. Say it at noon. Say it at night. Say it each hour of every day. Say it to yourself until the words stand out like letters of fire across the sky.

"Impress yourself with the idea. Fill yourself with the thought. Then take whatever portion seems wise. Let it be not less than one-tenth and lay it by. Arrange your other expenditures to do this if necessary. But lay by that portion first. Soon you will realize what a rich feeling it is to own a treasure upon which you alone have claim. As it grows it will stimulate you. A new joy of life will thrill you. Greater efforts will come to you to earn more. For of your increased earnings, will not the same percentage be also yours to keep?

"Then learn to make your treasure work for you. Make it your slave. Make its children and its children's children work for you.

"Insure an income for thy future. Look thou at the aged and forget not that in the days to come thou also will be numbered among them. Therefore invest thy treasure with greatest caution that it be not lost. Usurious rates of return are deceitful sirens that sing but to lure the unwary upon the rocks of loss and remorse.

"Provide also that thy family may not want should the gods call thee to their realms. For such protection it is always possible to make provision with small payments at regular intervals. Therefore the provident man delays not in expectation of a large sum becoming available for such a wise purpose.

"Counsel with wise men. Seek the advice of men whose daily work is handling money. Let them save you from such an error as I myself made in entrusting my money to the judgment of Azmur, the brickmaker. A small return and a safe one is far more desirable than risk.

"Enjoy life while you are here. Do not overstrain or try to save too much. If one-tenth of all you earn is as much as you can comfortably keep, be content to keep this portion. Live otherwise according to your income and let not yourself get niggardly and afraid to spend. Life is good and life is rich with things worthwhile and things to enjoy."

His friends thanked him and went away. Some were silent because they had no imagination and could not understand. Some were sarcastic because they thought that one so rich should divide with old friends not so fortunate. But some had in their eyes a new light. They realized that Algamish had come back each time to the room of the scribes because he was watching a man work his way out of darkness into light. When that man had found the light, a place awaited him. No one could fill that place until he had for himself worked out his own understanding, until he was ready for opportunity.

These latter were the ones, who, in the following years, frequently revisited Arkad, who received them gladly. He counseled with them and gave them freely of his wisdom as men of broad experience are always glad to do. And he assisted them in so investing their savings that it would bring in a good interest with safety and would neither be lost nor entangled in investments that paid no dividends.

The turning point in these men's lives came upon that day when they realized the truth that had come from Algamish to Arkad and from Arkad to them.

3. Seven Cures for a Lean Purse

The glory of Babylon endures. Down through the ages its reputation comes to us as the richest of cities, its treasures as fabulous.

Yet it was not always so. The riches of Babylon were the results of the wisdom of its people. They first had to learn how to become wealthy.

When the good king, Sargon, returned to Babylon after defeating his enemies, the Elamites, he was confronted with a serious situation. The Royal Chancellor explained it to the king thus:

"After many years of great prosperity brought to our people because your majesty built the great irrigation canals and the mighty temples of the Gods, now that these works are completed the people seem unable to support themselves.

"The laborers are without employment. The merchants have few customers. The farmers are unable to sell their produce. The people have not enough gold to buy food."

"But where has all the gold gone that we spent for these great improvements?" demanded the King.

"It has found its way, I fear," responded the Chancellor, "into the possession of a few very rich men of our city. It filtered through the fingers of most our people as quickly as the goat's milk goes through the strainer. Now that the stream of gold has ceased to flow, most of our people have nothing to show for their earnings."

The King was thoughtful for some time. Then he asked, "Why should so few men be able to acquire all the gold?"

"Because they know how," replied the Chancellor. "One may not condemn a man for succeeding because he knows how. Neither may one with justice take away from a man what he has fairly earned, to give to men of less ability."

"But why," demanded the King, "should not all the people learn how to accumulate gold and therefore become themselves rich and prosperous?"

"Quite possible, your excellency. But who can teach them? Certainly not the priests, because they know naught of money making."

"Who knows best in all our city how to become wealthy, Chancellor?" asked the King.

"Thy question answers itself, your majesty. Who has amassed the greatest wealth, in Babylon?"

"Well said, my able Chancellor. It is Arkad. He is the richest man in

Babylon. Bring him before me on the morrow."

Upon the following day, as the King had decreed, Arkad appeared before him, straight and sprightly despite his three score years and ten.

"Arkad," spoke the King, "is it true thou art the richest man in Babylon?"

"So it is reported, your majesty, and no man disputes it"

"How becamest thou so wealthy?"

"By taking advantage of opportunities available to all citizens of our good city."

"Thou hadst nothing to start with?"

"Only a great desire for wealth. Besides this, nothing."

"Arkad," continued the King, "our city is in a very unhappy state because a few men know how to acquire wealth and therefore monopolize it, while the mass of our citizens lack the knowledge of how to keep any part of the gold they receive.

"It is my desire that Babylon be the wealthiest city in the world. Therefore, it must be a city of many wealthy men. Therefore, we must teach all the people how to acquire riches. Tell me, Arkad, is there any secret to acquiring wealth? Can it be taught?"

"It is practical, your majesty. That which one man knows can be taught to others."

The king's eyes glowed. "Arkad, thou speaketh the words I wish to hear. Wilt thou lend thyself to this great cause? Wilt thou teach thy knowledge to a school for teachers, each of whom shall teach others until there are enough trained to teach these truths to every worthy subject in my domain?"

Arkad bowed and said, "I am thy humble servant to command. Whatever knowledge I possess will I gladly give for the betterment of my fellowmen and the glory of my King. Let your good chancellor arrange for me a class of one hundred men and I will teach to them those seven cures which did fatten my purse, than which there was none leaner in all Babylon."

A fortnight later, in compliance with the King's command, the chosen hundred assembled in the great hall of the Temple of Learning, seated upon colorful rings in a semicircle. Arkad sat beside a small taboret upon which smoked a sacred lamp sending forth a strange and pleasing odor.

"Behold the richest man in Babylon," whispered a student, nudging his neighbor as Arkad arose. "He is but a man even as the rest of us."

"As a dutiful subject of our great King," Arkad began, "I stand before you in his service. Because once I was a poor youth who did greatly desire gold, and because I found knowledge that enabled me to acquire it, he asks that I impart unto you my knowledge.

"I started my fortune in the humblest way. I had no advantage not enjoyed as fully by you and every citizen in Babylon.

"The first storehouse of my treasure was a well-purse. I loathed its useless emptiness. I desired it be round and full, clinking with the sound of gold. Therefore, I sought every remedy for a lean purse. I found seven.

"To you, who are assembled before me, shall I explain the seven cures for a lean purse which I do recommend to all men who desire much gold. Each day for seven days will I explain to you one of the seven remedies.

"Listen attentively to the knowledge that I will impart. Debate it with me. Discuss it among yourselves. Learn these lessons thoroughly, that ye may also plant in your own purse the seed of wealth. First must each of you start wisely to build a fortune of his own. Then wilt thou be competent, and only then, to teach these truths to others.

"I shall teach to you in simple ways how to fatten your purses. This is the first step leading to the temple of wealth, and no man may climb who cannot plant his feet firmly upon the first step.

"We shall now consider the first cure."

THE FIRST CURE: Start thy purse to fattening

Arkad addressed a thoughtful man in the second row. "My good friend, at what craft workest thou?"

"I," replied the man, "am a scribe and carve records upon the clay tablets."

"Even at such labor did I myself earn my first coppers. Therefore, thou hast the same opportunity to build a fortune."

He spoke to a florid-faced man, farther back. "Pray tell also what dost thou to earn thy bread?"

"I," responded this man, "am a meat butcher. I do buy the goats the farmers raise and kill them and sell the meat to the housewives and the hides to the sandal-makers."

"Because thou dost also labor and earn, thou hast every advantage to succeed that I did possess."

In this way did Arkad proceed to find out how each man labored to earn his living. When he had done questioning them, he said:

"Now, my students, ye can see that there are many trades and labors at which men may earn coins. Each of the ways of earning is a stream of gold from which the worker doth divert by his labors a portion to his own purse. Therefore into the purse of each of you flows a stream of coins large or small according to his ability. Is it not so?"

Thereupon they agreed that it was so.

"Then," continued Arkad, "if each of you desireth to build for himself a fortune, is it not wise to start by utilizing that source of wealth which he already has established?"

To this they agreed.

Then Arkad turned to a humble man who had declared himself an egg merchant. "If thou select one of thy baskets and put into it each morning ten eggs and take out from it each evening nine eggs, what will eventually happen?"

"It will become in time overflowing."

"Why?"

"Because each day I put in one more egg than I take out."

Arkad turned to the class with a smile. "Does any man here have a lean purse?"

First they looked amused. Then they laughed. Lastly they waved their purses in jest.

"All right," he continued, "Now I shall tell thee the first remedy I learned to cure a lean purse. Do exactly as I have suggested to the egg merchant. *For every ten coins thou placest within thy purse take out for use but nine. Thy purse will start to fatten at once and its increasing weight will feel good in thy hand and bring satisfaction to thy soul.*

"Deride not what I say because of its simplicity. Truth is always simple. I told thee I would tell how I built my fortune. This was my beginning. I, too, carried a lean purse and cursed it because there was naught within to satisfy my desires. But when I began to take out from my purse but nine parts of ten I put in, it began to fatten. So will thine.

"Now I will tell a strange truth, the reason for which I know not. When I ceased to pay out more than nine-tenths of my earnings, I managed to get along just as well. I was not shorter than before. Also, ere long, did coins come to me more easily than before. Surely it is a law of the gods that unto him who keepeth and spendeth not a certain part of all his earnings, shall gold come more easily. Likewise, him whose purse is empty does gold avoid.

"Which desirest thou the most? Is it the gratification of thy desires of each day, a jewel, a bit of finery, better raiment, more food; things quickly gone and forgotten? Or is it substantial belongings, gold, lands, herds, merchandise, income-bringing investments? The coins thou takest from thy purse bring the first. The coins thou leavest within it will bring the latter.

"This, my students, was the first cure I did discover for my lean purse: *'For each ten coins I put in, to spend but nine.'* Debate this amongst yourselves. If any man proves it untrue, tell me upon the morrow when we shall meet again."

THE SECOND CURE: Control thy expenditures

"Some of your members, my students, have asked me this: 'How can a man keep one-tenth of all he earns in his purse when all the coins he earns are not enough for his necessary expenses?' " So did Arkad address his students upon the second day.

"Yesterday how many of thee carried lean purses?"

"All of us," answered the class.

"Yet, thou do not all earn the same. Some earn much more than others. Some have much larger families to support. Yet, all purses were equally lean. Now I will tell thee an unusual truth about men and sons of men. It is this: That what each of us calls our 'necessary expenses' will always grow to equal our incomes unless we protest to the contrary.

"Confuse not the necessary expenses with thy desires. Each of you, together with your good families, have more desires than your earnings can gratify. Therefore are thy earnings spent to gratify these desires insofar as they will go. Still thou retainest many ungratified desires.

"All men are burdened with more desires than they can gratify. Because of my wealth thinkest thou I may gratify every desire? 'Tis a false idea. There are limits to my time. There are limits to my strength. There are limits to the distance I may travel. There are limits to what I may eat. There are limits to the zest with which I may enjoy.

"I say to you that just as weeds grow in a field wherever the farmer leaves space for their roots, even so freely do desires grow in men whenever there is a possibility of their being gratified. Thy desires are a multitude and those that thou mayest gratify are but few.

"Study thoughtfully thy accustomed habits of living. Herein may be most often found certain accepted expenses that may wisely be reduced or eliminated. Let thy motto be one hundred percent of appreciated value demanded for each coin spent.

"Therefore, engrave upon the clay each thing for which thou desireth to spend. Select those that are necessary and others that are possible through the expenditure of nine-tenths of thy income. Cross out the rest and consider them but a part of that great multitude of desires that must go unsatisfied and regret them not.

"Budget then thy necessary expenses. Touch not the one-tenth that is fattening thy purse. Let this be thy great desire that is being fulfilled. Keep working with thy budget, keep adjusting it to help thee. Make it thy first assistant in defending thy fattening purse."

Hereupon one of the students, wearing a robe of red and gold, arose and said, "I am a free man. I believe that it is my right to enjoy the good things of life. Therefore do I rebel against the slavery of a budget which determines just how much I may spend and for what. I feel it would take much pleasure from my life and make me little more than a pack-ass to carry a burden."

To him Arkad replied, "Who, my friend, would determine thy budget?"

"I would make it for myself," responded the protesting one.

"In that case were a pack-ass to budget his burden would he include therein jewels and rugs and heavy bars of gold? Not so. He would include hay and grain and a bag of water for the desert trail.

"The purpose of a budget is to help thy purse to fatten. It is to assist thee to have thy necessities and, insofar as attainable, thy other desires. It is to enable thee to realize thy most cherished desires by defending them from thy casual wishes. Like a bright light in a dark cave thy budget shows up the leaks from thy purse and enables thee to stop them and control thy expenditures for definite and gratifying purposes.

"This, then, is the second cure for a lean purse. *Budget thy expenses that thou mayest have coins to pay for thy necessities, to pay for thy enjoyments and to gratify thy worthwhile desires without spending more than nine-tenths of thy earnings*."

THE THIRD CURE: Make thy gold multiply

"Behold thy lean purse is fattening. Thou hast disciplined thyself to leave therein one-tenth of all thou earneth. Thou hast controlled thy expenditures to protect thy growing treasure. Next, we will consider means to put thy treasure to labor and to increase. Gold in a purse is gratifying to own and satisfieth a miserly soul but earns nothing. The gold we may retain from our earnings is but the start. The earnings it will make shall build our fortunes." So spoke Arkad upon the third day to his class.

"How therefore may we put our gold to work? My first investment was unfortunate, for I lost all. Its tale I will relate later. My first profitable investment was a loan I made to a man named Aggar, a shield maker. Once each year did he buy large shipments of bronze brought from across the sea to use in his trade. Lacking sufficient capital to pay the merchants, he would borrow from those who had extra coins. He was an honorable man. His borrowing he would repay, together with a liberal rental, as he sold his shields.

"Each time I loaned to him I loaned back also the rental he had paid to me. Therefore not only did my capital increase, but its earnings likewise increased. Most gratifying was it to have these sums return to my purse.

"I tell you, my students, a man's wealth is not in the coins he carries in his purse; it is the income he buildeth, the golden stream that continually floweth into his purse and keepeth it always bulging. That is what every man desireth. That is what thou, each one of thee desireth; an income that continueth to come whether thou work or travel.

"Great income I have acquired. So great that I am called a very rich man. My loans to Aggar were my first training in profitable investment. Gaining wisdom from this experience, I extended my loans and investments as my capital increased. From a few sources at first, from many sources later, flowed into my purse a golden stream of wealth available for such wise uses as I should decide.

"Behold, from my humble earnings I had begotten a hoard of golden slaves, each laboring and earning more gold. As they labored for me, so their children also labored and their children's children until great was the income from their combined efforts.

"Gold increaseth rapidly when making reasonable earnings as thou wilt see from the following: A farmer, when his first son was born, took ten pieces of silver to a money lender and asked him to keep it on rental for his son until he became twenty years of age. This the money lender did, and agreed the rental should be one-fourth of its value each four years. The farmer asked, because this sum he had set aside as belonging to his son, that the rental be add to the principal.

"When the boy had reached the age of twenty years, the farmer again went to the money lender to inquire about the silver. The money lender explained that because this sum had been increased by compound interest, the original ten pieces of silver had now grown to thirty and one-half pieces.

"The farmer was well pleased and because the son did not need the coins, he left them with the money lender. When the son became fifty years of age, the father meantime having passed to the other world, the money lender paid the son in settlement one hundred and sixty-seven pieces of silver.

"Thus in fifty years had the investment multiplied itself at rental almost seventeen times.

"This, then, is the third cure for a lean purse: *to put each coin to laboring that it may reproduce its kind even as the flocks of the field and help bring to thee income, a stream of wealth that shall flow constantly into thy purse.*"

THE FOURTH CURE: Guard thy treasures from loss

"Misfortune loves a shining mark. Gold in a man's purse must be guarded with firmness, else it be lost. Thus it is wise that we must first secure small amounts and learn to protect them before the gods entrust us with larger." So spoke Arkad upon the fourth day to his class.

"Every owner of gold is tempted by opportunities whereby it would seem that he could make large sums by its investment in most plausible projects. Often friends and relatives are eagerly entering such investment and urge him to follow.

"The first sound principle of investment is security for thy principal. Is it wise to be intrigued by larger earnings when thy principal may be lost? I say not. The penalty of risk is probable loss. Study carefully, before parting with thy treasure, each assurance that it may be safely reclaimed. Be not misled by thine own romantic desires to make wealth rapidly.

"Before thou loan it to any man assure thyself of his ability to repay and his reputation for doing so, that thou mayest not unwittingly be making him a present of thy hard-earned treasure.

"Before thou entrust it as an investment in any field acquaint thyself with the dangers which may beset it.

"My own first investment was a tragedy to me at the time. The guarded savings of a year I did entrust to a brickmaker, named Azmur, who was traveling over the far seas and in Tyre agreed to buy for me the rare jewels of the Phoenicians. These we would sell upon his return and divide the profits. The Phoenicians were scoundrels and sold him bits of glass. My treasure was lost. Today, my training would show to me at once the folly of entrusting a brickmaker to buy jewels.

"Therefore, do I advise thee from the wisdom of my experiences: be not too confident of thine own wisdom in entrusting thy treasures to the possible pitfalls of investments. Better by far to consult the wisdom of those experienced in handling money for profit. Such advice is freely given for the asking and may readily possess a value equal in gold to the sum thou considerest investing. In truth, such is its actual value if it save thee from loss.

"This, then, is the fourth cure for a lean purse, and of great importance if it prevent thy purse from being emptied once it has become well filled. *Guard thy treasure from loss by investing only where thy principal is safe, where it may be reclaimed if desirable, and where thou will not fail to collect a fair rental. Consult with wise men. Secure the advice of those experienced in the profitable handling of gold. Let their wisdom protect thy treasure from unsafe investments.*"

THE FIFTH CURE: Make of thy dwelling a profitable investment

"If a man setteth aside nine parts of his earnings upon which to live and enjoy life, and if any part of this nine parts he can turn into a profitable investment without detriment to his well-being, then so much faster will his treasures grow." So spoke Arkad to his class at their fifth lesson.

"All too many of our men of Babylon do raise their families in unseemly quarters. They do pay to exacting landlords liberal rentals for rooms where their wives have not a spot to raise the blooms that gladden a woman's heart and their children have no place to play their games except in the unclean alleys.

"No man's family can fully enjoy life unless they do have a plot of ground wherein children can play in the clean earth and where the wife may raise not only blossoms but good rich herbs to feed her family.

"To a man's heart it brings gladness to eat the figs from his own trees and the grapes of his own vines. To own his own domicile and to have it a place he is proud to care for, putteth confidence in his heart and greater effort behind all his endeavors. Therefore, do I recommend that every man own the roof that sheltereth him and his.

"Nor is it beyond the ability of any well intentioned man to own his home. Hath not our great king so widely extended the walls of Babylon that within them much land is now unused and may be purchased at sums most reasonable?

"Also I say to you, my students, that the money lenders gladly consider the desires of men who seek homes and land for their families. Readily may thou borrow to pay the brickmaker and the builder for such commendable purposes, if thou can show a reasonable portion of the necessary sum which thou thyself hath provided for the purpose.

"Then when the house be built, thou canst pay the money lender with the same regularity as thou didst pay the landlord. Because each payment will reduce thy indebtedness to the money lender, a few years will satisfy his loan.

"Then will thy heart be glad because thou wilt own in thy own right a valuable property and thy only cost will be the king's taxes.

"Also wilt thy good wife go more often to the river to wash thy robes, that each time returning she may bring a goatskin of water to pour upon the growing things.

"Thus come many blessings to the man who owneth his own house. And greatly will it reduce his cost of living, making available more of his earnings for pleasures and the gratification of his desires. This, then, is the fifth cure for a lean purse: *Own thy own home*"

THE SIXTH CURE: Insure a future income

"The life of every man proceedeth from his childhood to his old age. This is the path of life and no man may deviate from it unless the gods call him prematurely to the world beyond. Therefore do I say that it *behooves a man to make preparation for a suitable income in the days to come,* when he is no longer young, and *to make preparations for his family should he be no longer with them to comfort and support them.* This lesson shall instruct thee in providing a full purse when time has made thee less able to learn." So Arkad addressed his class upon the sixth day.

"The man who, because of his understanding of the laws of wealth, acquireth a growing surplus, should give thought to those future days. He should plan certain investments or provision that may endure safely for many years, yet will be available when the time arrives which he has so wisely anticipated.

"There are diverse ways by which a man may provide with safety for his future. He may provide a hiding place and there bury a secret treasure. Yet, no matter with what skill it be hidden, it may nevertheless become the loot of thieves. For this reason I recommend not this plan.

"A man may buy houses or lands for this purpose. If wisely chosen as to their usefulness and value in the future, they are permanent in their value and their earnings or their sale will provide well for his purpose.

"A man may loan a small sum to the money lender and increase it at regular periods. The rental which the money lender adds to this will largely add to its increase. I do know a sandal maker, named Ansan, who explained to me not long ago that each week for eight years he had deposited with his money lender two pieces of silver. The money lender had but recently given him an accounting over which he greatly rejoiced. The total of his small deposits with their rental at the customary rate of one-fourth their value for each four years, had now become a thousand and forty pieces of silver.

"I did gladly encourage him further by demonstrating to him with my knowledge of the numbers that in twelve years more, if he would keep his regular deposits of but two pieces of silver each week, the money lender would then owe him four thousand pieces of silver, a worthy competence for the rest of his life.

"Surely, when such a small payment made with regularity doth produce such profitable results, *no man can afford not to insure a treasure for his old age and the protection of his family, no matter how prosperous his business and his investments may be.*

"I would that I might say more about this. In my mind rests a belief that someday wise-thinking men will devise a plan to insure against death whereby many men pay in but a trifling sum regularly, the aggregate making a handsome sum for the family of each member who passeth to the beyond. This do I see as something desirable and which I could highly recommend. But today it is not possible because it must reach beyond the life of any man or any partnership to operate. It must be as stable as the king's throne. Someday do I feel that such a plan shall come to pass and be a great blessing to many men, because even the first small payment will make available a snug fortune for the family of a member should he pass on.

"But because we live in our own day and not in the days which are to come, must we take advantage of those means and ways of accomplishing our purposes. Therefore do I recommend to all men, that they, by wise and well thought out methods, do provide against a lean purse in their mature years. For a lean purse to a man no longer able to earn or to a family without its head is a sore tragedy.

"This, then, is the sixth cure for a lean purse. *Provide in advance for the needs of thy growing age and the protection of thy family."*

THE SEVENTH CURE: Increase thy ability to earn

"This day do I speak to thee, my students, of one of the most vital remedies for a lean purse. Yet, I will talk not of gold but of yourselves, of the men beneath the robes of many colors who do sit before me. I will talk to you of those things within the minds and lives of men which do work for or against their success." So did Arkad address his class upon the seventh day.

"Not long ago came to me a young man seeking to borrow. When I questioned him the cause of his necessity, he complained that his earnings were insufficient to pay his expenses. Thereupon I explained to him, this being the case, he was a poor customer for the money lender, as he possessed no surplus earning capacity to repay the loan.

" 'What you need, young man,' I told him, 'is to earn more coins. What dost thou to increase thy capacity to earn?'

" 'All that I can do' he replied. 'Six times within two moons have I approached my master to request my pay be increased, but without success. No man can go oftener than that.'

"We may smile at his simplicity, yet he did possess one of the vital requirements to increase his earnings. Within him was a strong desire to earn more, a proper and commendable desire.

"Preceding accomplishment must be desire. Thy desires must be strong and definite. General desires are but weak longings. For a man to wish to be rich is of little purpose. For a man to desire five pieces of gold is a tangible desire which he can press to fulfillment. After he has backed his desire for five pieces of gold with strength of purpose to secure it, next he can find similar ways to obtain ten pieces and then twenty pieces and later a thousand pieces and, behold, he has become wealthy. In learning to secure his one definite small desire, he hath trained himself to secure a larger one. This is the process by which wealth is accumulated: first in small sums, then in larger ones as a man learns and becomes more capable.

"Desires must be simple and definite. They defeat their own purpose should they be too many, too confusing, or beyond a man's training to accomplish.

"As a man perfecteth himself in his calling even so doth his ability to earn increase. In those days when I was a humble scribe carving upon the clay for a few coppers each day, I observed that other workers did more than I and were paid more. Therefore, did I determine that I would be exceeded by none. Nor did it take long for me to discover the reason for their greater success. More interest in my work, more concentration upon my task, more persistence in my effort, and, behold, few men could carve more tablets in a day than I. With reasonable promptness my increased skill was rewarded, nor was it necessary for me to go six times to my master to request recognition.

"The more of wisdom we know, the more we may earn. That man who seeks to learn more of his craft shall be richly rewarded. If he is an artisan, he may seek to learn the methods and the tools of those most skillful in the same line. If he laboreth at the law or at healing, he may consult and exchange knowledge with others of his calling. If he be a merchant, he may continually seek better goods that can be purchased at lower prices.

"Always do the affairs of man change and improve because keen-minded men seek greater skill that they may better serve those upon whose patronage they depend. Therefore, I urge all men to be in the front rank of progress and not to stand still, lest they be left behind.

"Many things come to make a man's life rich with gainful experiences. Such things as the following, a man must do if he respect himself:

"He must pay his debts with all the promptness within his power, not purchasing that for which he is unable to pay.

"He must take care of his family that they may think and speak well of him.

"He must make a will of record that, in case the gods call him, proper and honorable division of his property be accomplished.

"He must have compassion upon those who are injured and smitten by misfortune and aid them within reasonable limits. He must do deeds of thoughtfulness to those dear to him.

"Thus the seventh and last remedy for a lean purse is to *cultivate thy own powers, to study and become wiser, to become more skillful, to so act as to respect thyself.* Thereby shalt thou acquire confidence in thy self to achieve thy carefully considered desires.

"These then are the seven cures for a lean purse, which, out of the experience of a long and successful life, I do urge for all men who desire wealth.

"There is more gold in Babylon, my students, than thou dreamest of. There is abundance for all.

"Go thou forth and practice these truths that thou mayest prosper and grow wealthy, as is thy right.

"Go thou forth and teach these truths that every honorable subject of his majesty may also share liberally in the ample wealth of our beloved city."

4. Meet the Goddess of Good Luck

"If a man be lucky, there is no foretelling the possible extent of his good fortune. Pitch him into the Euphrates and like as not he will swim out with a pearl in his hand." —Babylonian Proverb

The desire to be lucky is universal. It was just as strong in the breasts of men four thousand years ago in ancient Babylon as it is in the hearts of men today. We all hope to be favored by the whimsical Goddess of Good Luck. Is there some way we can meet her and attract, not only her favorable attention, but her generous favors?

Is there a way to attract good luck?

That is just what the men of ancient Babylon wished to know. It is exactly what they decided to find out. They were shrewd men and keen thinkers. That explains why their city became the richest and most powerful city of their time.

In that distant past, they had no schools or colleges. Nevertheless they had a center of learning and a very practical one it was. Among the towered buildings in Babylon was one that ranked in importance with the Palace of the King, the Hanging Gardens and the temples of the Gods. You will find scant mention of it in the history books, more likely no mention at all, yet it exerted a powerful influence upon the thought of that time.

This building was the Temple of Learning where the wisdom of the past was expounded by voluntary teachers and where subjects of popular interest were discussed in open forums. Within its walls all men met as equals. The humblest of slaves could dispute with impunity the opinions of a prince of the royal house.

Among the many who frequented the Temple of Learning, was a wise rich man named Arkad, called the richest man in Babylon. He had his own special hall where almost any evening a large group of men, some old, some very young, but mostly middle-aged, gathered to discuss and argue interesting subjects. Suppose we listen in to see whether they knew how to attract good luck.

The sun had just set like a great red ball of fire shining through the haze of desert dust when Arkad strolled to his accustomed platform. Already full four score men were awaiting his arrival, reclining on their small rugs spread upon the floor. More were still arriving.

"What shall we discuss this night?" Arkad inquired.

After a brief hesitation, a tall cloth weaver addressed him, arising as was the custom. "I have a subject I would like to hear discussed yet hesitate to offer lest it seem ridiculous to you, Arkad, and my good friends here."

Upon being urged to offer it, both by Arkad and by calls from the others, he continued: "This day I have been lucky, for I have found a purse in which there are pieces of gold. To continue to be lucky is my great desire. Feeling that all men share with me this desire, I do suggest we debate how to attract good luck that we may discover ways it can be enticed to one."

"A most interesting subject has been offered," Arkad commented, "one most worthy of our discussion. To some men, good luck bespeaks but a chance happening that, like an accident, may befall one without purpose or reason. Others do believe that the instigator of all good fortune is our most bounteous goddess, Ashtar, ever anxious to reward with generous gifts those who please her. Speak up, my friends, what say you, shall we seek to find if there be means by which good luck may be enticed to visit each and all of us?"

"Yea! Yea! And much of it!" responded the growing group of eager listeners.

Thereupon Arkad continued, "To start our discussion, let us first hear from those among us who have enjoyed experiences similar to that of the cloth weaver in finding or receiving, without effort upon their part, valuable treasures or jewels."

There was a pause in which all looked about expecting someone to reply but no one did.

"What, no one?" Arkad said, "Then rare indeed must be this kind of good luck. Who now will offer a suggestion as to where we shall continue our search?"

"That I will do," spoke a well-robed young man, arising. "When a man speaketh of luck is it not natural that his thoughts turn to the gaining tables? Is it not there we find many men courting the favor of the goddess in hope she will bless them with rich winnings?"

As he resumed his seat a voice called, "Do not stop! Continue thy story! Tell us, didst thou find favor with the goddess at the gaming tables? Did she turn the cubes with red side up so thou filled thy purse at the dealer's expense or did she permit the blue sides to come up so the dealer raked in thy hard-earned pieces of silver?"

The young man joined the good-natured laughter, then replied, "I am not averse to admitting she seemed not to know I was even there. But how about the rest of you? Have you found her waiting about such places to roll the cubes, in your favor? We are eager to hear as well as to learn."

"A wise start," broke in Arkad. "We meet here to consider all sides of each question. To ignore the gaming table would be to overlook an instinct common to most men, the love of taking a chance with a small amount of silver in the hope of winning much gold."

"That doth remind me of the races but yesterday," called out another listener. "If the goddess frequents the gaming tables, certainly she dost not overlook the races where the gilded chariots and the foaming horses offer far more excitement. Tell us honestly, Arkad, didst she whisper to you to place your bet upon those grey horses from Nineveh yesterday? I was standing just behind thee and could scarce believe my ears when I heard thee place thy bet upon the greys. Thou knowest as well as any of us that no team in all Assyria can beat our beloved bays in a fair race.

"Didst the goddess whisper in thy ear to bet upon the greys because at the last turn the inside black would stumble and so interfere with our bays that the greys would win the race and score an unearned victory?"

Arkad smiled indulgently at the banter. "What reason have we to feel the good goddess would take that much interest in any man's bet upon a horse race? To me she is a goddess of love and dignity whose pleasure it is to aid those who are in need and to reward those who are deserving. I look to find her, not at the gaming tables or the races where men lose more gold than they win but in other places where the doings of men are more worthwhile and more worthy of reward.

"In tilling the soil, in honest trading, in all of man's occupations, there is opportunity to make a profit upon his efforts and his transactions. Perhaps not all the time will he be rewarded because sometimes his judgment may be faulty and other times the winds and the weather may defeat his efforts. Yet, if he persists, he may usually expect to realize his profit. This is so because the chances of profit are always in his favor.

"But, when a man playeth the games, the situation is reversed for the chances of profit are always against him and always in favor of the game keeper. The game is so arranged that it will always favor the keeper. It is his business at which he plans to make a liberal profit for himself from the coins bet by the players. Few players realize how certain are the game keeper's profits and how uncertain are their own chances to win.

"For example, let us consider wagers placed upon the cube. Each time it is cast we bet which side will be uppermost. If it be the red side the game master pays to us four times our bet. But if any other of the five sides come uppermost, we lose our bet. Thus the figures show that for each cast we have five chances to lose, but because the red pays four for one, we have four chances to win. In a night's play the game master can expect to keep for his profit one-fifth of all the coins wagered. Can a man expect to win more than occasionally against odds so arranged that he should lose one-fifth of all his bets?"

"Yet some men do win large sums at times," volunteered one of the listeners.

"Quite so, they do," Arkad continued. "Realizing this, the question comes to me whether money secured in such ways brings permanent value to those who are thus lucky. Among my acquaintances are many of the successful men of Babylon, yet among them I am unable to name a single one who started his success from such a source.

"You who are gathered here tonight know many more of our substantial citizens. To me it would be of much interest to learn how many of our successful citizens can credit the gaming tables with their start to success. Suppose each of you tell of those you know. What say you?"

After a prolonged silence, a wag ventured, "Wouldst thy inquiry include the game keepers?"

"If you think of no one else," Arkad responded. "If not one of you can think of anyone else, then how about yourselves? Are there any consistent winners with us who hesitate to advise such a source for their incomes?"

His challenge was answered by a series of groans from the rear taken up and spread amid much laughter.

"It would seem we are not seeking good luck in such places as the goddess frequents," he continued. "Therefore let us explore other fields. We have not found it in picking up lost wallets. Neither have we found it haunting the gaming tables. As to the races, I must confess to have lost far more coins there than I have ever won.

"Now, suppose we consider our trades and businesses. Is it not natural if we conclude a profitable transaction to consider it not good luck but a just reward for our efforts? I am inclined to think we may be overlooking the gifts of the goddess. Perhaps she really does assist us when we do not appreciate her generosity. Who can suggest further discussion?"

Thereupon an elderly merchant arose, smoothing his genteel white robe. "With thy permission, most honorable Arkad and my friends, I offer a suggestion. If, as you have said, we take credit to our own industry and ability for our business success, why not consider the successes we almost enjoyed but which escaped us, happenings which would have been most profitable. They would have been rare examples of good luck if they had actually happened. Because they were not brought to fulfillment we cannot consider them as our just rewards. Surely many men here have such experiences to relate."

"Here is a wise approach," Arkad approved. "Who among you have had good luck within your grasp only to see it escape?"

Many hands were raised, among them that of the merchant. Arkad motioned to him to speak. "As you suggested this approach, we should like to hear first from you."

"I will gladly relate a tale," he resumed, "that doth illustrate how closely unto a man good luck may approach and how blindly he may permit it to escape, much to his loss and later regret.

"Many years ago, when I was a young man, just married and well-started to earning, my father did come one day and urge most strongly that I enter in an investment. The son of one of his good friends had taken notice of a barren tract of land not far beyond the outer walls of our city. It lay high above the canal where no water could reach it.

"The son of my father's friend devised a plan to purchase this land, build three large water wheels that could be operated by oxen and thereby raise the life-giving waters to the fertile soil. This accomplished, he planned to divide into small tracts and sell to the residents of the city for herb patches.

"The son of my father's friend did not possess sufficient gold to complete such an undertaking. Like myself, he was a young man earning a fair sum. His father, like mine, was a man of large family and small means. He, therefore, decided to interest a group of men to enter the enterprise with him. The group was to comprise twelve, each of whom must be a money earner and agree to pay one-tenth of his earnings into the enterprise until the land was made ready for sale. All would then share justly in the profits in proportion to their investment.

" 'Thou, my son,' bespoke my father unto me, 'art now in thy young manhood. It is my deep desire that thou begin the building of a valuable estate for myself that thou mayest become respected among men. I desire to see thou profit from a knowledge of the thoughtless mistakes of thy father.'

" 'This do I most ardently desire, my father,' I replied.

" 'Then, this do I advise. Do what I should have done at thy age. From thy earnings keep out one-tenth to put into favorable investments. With this one-tenth of thy earnings and what it will also earn, thou canst, before thou art my age, accumulate for thyself a valuable estate.'

" 'Thy words are words of wisdom, my father. Greatly do I desire riches. Yet there are many uses to which my earnings are called. Therefore, do I hesitate to do as thou dost advise. I am young. There is plenty of time.'

" 'So I thought at thy age, yet behold, many years have passed and I have not yet made the beginning.'

" 'We live in a different age, my father. I shall avoid thy mistakes.'

" 'Opportunity stands before thee, my son. It is offering a chance that may lead to wealth. I beg of thee, do not delay. Go upon the morrow to the son of my friend and bargain with him to pay ten percent of thy earnings into this investment. Go promptly upon the morrow. Opportunity waits for no man.

Today it is here; soon it is gone. Therefore, delay not!'

"In spite of the advice of my father, I did hesitate. There were beautiful new robes just brought by the tradesmen from the East, robes of such richness and beauty my good wife and I felt we must each possess one. Should I agree to pay one-tenth of my earnings into the enterprise, we must deprive ourselves of these and other pleasures we dearly desired. I delayed making a decision until it was too late, much to my subsequent regret. The enterprise did prove to be more profitable than any man had prophesied. This is my tale, showing how I did permit good luck to escape."

"In this tale we see how *good luck waits to come to that man who accepts opportunity*," commented a swarthy man of the desert. "To the building of an estate there must always be the beginning. That start may be a few pieces of gold or silver which a man diverts from his earnings to his first investment. I, myself, am the owner of many herds. The start of my herds I did begin when I was a mere boy and did purchase with one piece of silver a young calf. This, being the beginning of my wealth, was of great importance to me.

"To take his first start to building an estate is as good luck as can come to any man. With all men, that first step, which changes them from men who earn from their own labor to men who draw dividends from the earnings of their gold, is important. Some, fortunately, take it when young and thereby outstrip in financial success those who do take it later or those unfortunate men, like the father of this merchant, who never take it.

"Had our friend, the merchant, taken this step in his early manhood when this opportunity came to him, this day he would be blessed with much more of this world's goods. Should the good luck of our friend, the cloth weaver, cause him to take such a step at this time, it will indeed be but the beginning of much greater good fortune."

"Thank you! I like to speak, also." A stranger from another country arose. "I am a Syrian. Not so well do I speak your tongue. I wish to call this friend, the merchant, a name. Maybe you think it not polite, this name. Yet I wish to call him that. But, alas, I not know your word for it. If I do call it in Syrian, you will not understand. Therefore, please some good gentlemen, tell me that right name you call man who puts off doing those things that mighty good for him."

"Procrastinator," called a voice.

"That's him," shouted the Syrian, waving his hands excitedly, "he accepts not opportunity when she comes. He waits. He says I have much business right now. Bye and bye I talk to you. Opportunity, she will not wait for such slow fellow. She thinks if a man desires to be lucky he will step quick. Any man not step quick when opportunity comes, he big procrastinator like our friend, this merchant."

The merchant arose and bowed good naturedly in response to the laughter. "My admiration to thee, stranger within our gates, who hesitates not to speak the truth."

"And now let us hear another tale of opportunity. Who has for us another experience?" demanded Arkad.

"I have," responded a red-robed man of middle age. "I am a buyer of animals, mostly camels and horses. Sometimes I do also buy the sheep and goats. The tale I am about to relate will tell truthfully how opportunity came one night when I did least expect it. Perhaps for this reason I did let it escape. Of this you shall be the judge.

"Returning to the city one evening after a disheartening ten-days' journey in search of camels, I was much angered to find the gates of the city closed and locked. While my slaves spread our tent for the night, which we looked to spend with little food and no I water, I was approached by an elderly farmer who, like ourselves, found himself locked outside.

" 'Honored sir,' he addressed me, 'from thy appearance, I do judge thee to be a buyer. If this be so, much would I like to sell to thee the most excellent flock of sheep just driven up. Alas, my good wife lies very sick with the fever. I must return with all haste. Buy thou my sheep that I and my slaves may mount our camels and travel back without delay."

"So dark it was that I could not see his flock, but from the bleating I did know it must be large. Having wasted ten days searching for camels I could not find, I was glad to bargain with him. In his anxiety, he did set a most reasonable price. I accepted, well knowing my slaves could drive the flock through the city gates in the morning and sell at a substantial profit.

"The bargain concluded, I called my slaves to bring torches that we might count the flock which the farmer declared to contain nine hundred. I shall not burden you, my friends, with a description of our difficulty in attempting to count so many thirsty, restless, milling sheep. It proved to be an impossible task. Therefore, I bluntly informed the farmer I would count them at daylight and pay him then.

" 'Please, most honorable sir,' he pleaded, 'pay me but two-thirds of the price tonight that I may be on my way. I will leave my most intelligent and educated slave to assist to make the count in the morning. He is trustworthy and to him thou canst pay the balance.'

"But I was stubborn and refused to make payment that night. Next morning, before I awoke, the city gates opened and four buyers rushed out in search of flocks. They were most eager and willing to pay high prices because the city was threatened with siege, and food was not plentiful. Nearly three times the price at which he had offered the flock to me did the old farmer receive for it. Thus was rare good luck allowed to escape."

"Here is a tale most unusual," commented Arkad. "What wisdom doth it suggest?"

"The wisdom of making a payment immediately when we are convinced our bargain is wise," suggested a venerable saddle maker. "If the bargain be good, then dost thou need protection against thy own weaknesses as much as against any other man. We mortals are changeable. Alas, I must say more apt to change our minds when right than wrong. Wrong, we are stubborn indeed. Right, we are prone to vacillate and let opportunity escape. My first judgment is my best. Yet always have I found it difficult to compel myself to proceed with a good bargain when made. Therefore, as a protection against my own weaknesses, I do make a prompt deposit thereon. This doth save me from later regrets for the good luck that should have been mine."

"Thank you! Again I like to speak." The Syrian was upon his feet once more. "These tales much alike. Each time opportunity fly away for same reason. Each time she come to procrastinator, bringing good plan. Each time they hesitate, not say, right now best time, I do it quick. How can men succeed that way?"

"Wise are thy words, my friend," responded the buyer. "Good luck fled from procrastination in both these tales. Yet, this is not unusual. The spirit of procrastination is within all men. We desire riches; yet, how often when opportunity doth appear before us, that spirit of procrastination from within doth urge various delays in our acceptance. In listening to it we do become our own worst enemies.

"In my younger days I did not know it by this long word our friend from Syria doth enjoy. I did think at first it was my own poor judgment that did cause me loss of many profitable trades. Later, I did credit it to my stubborn disposition. At last, I did recognize it for what it was—a habit of needless delaying where action was required, action prompt and decisive. How I did hate it when its true character stood revealed. With the bitterness of a wild ass hitched to a chariot, I did break loose from this enemy to my success."

"Thank you! I like ask question from Mr. Merchant." The Syrian was speaking. "You wear fine robes, not like those of poor man. You speak like successful man. Tell us, do you listen now when procrastination whispers in your ear?"

"Like our friend the buyer, I also had to recognize and conquer procrastination," responded the merchant. "To me, it proved to be an enemy, ever watching and waiting to thwart my accomplishments. The tale I did relate is but one of many similar instances I could tell to show how it drove away my opportunities. 'Tis not difficult to conquer, once understood. No man willingly permits the thief to rob his bins of grain. Nor does any man willingly permit an enemy to drive away his customers and rob him of his profits. When once I did recognize that such acts as these my enemy was committing, with determination I conquered him. So must every man master his own spirit of procrastination before he can expect to share in the rich treasures of Babylon.

"What sayest, Arkad? Because thou art the richest man in Babylon, many do proclaim thee to be the luckiest. Dost agree with me that no man can arrive at a full measure of success until he hath completely crushed the spirit of procrastination within him?"

"It is even as thou sayest," Arkad admitted. "During my long life I have watched generation following generation, marching forward along those avenues of trade, science and learning that lead to success in life. Opportunities came to all these men. Some grasped theirs and moved steadily to the gratification of their deepest desires, but the majority hesitated, faltered and fell behind."

Arkad turned to the cloth weaver. "Thou didst suggest that we debate good luck. Let us hear what thou now thinkest upon the subject."

"I do see good luck in a different light. I had thought of it as something most desirable that might happen to a man without effort upon his part. Now, I do realize such happenings are not the sort of thing one may attract to himself. From our discussion have I learned that *to attract good luck to oneself, it is necessary to take advantage of opportunities*. Therefore, in the future, I shall endeavor to make the best of such opportunities as do come to me."

"Thou hast well grasped the truths brought forth in our discussion," Arkad replied. "Good luck, we do find, often follows opportunity but seldom comes otherwise. Our merchant friend would have found great good luck had he accepted the opportunity the good goddess did present to him. Our friend the buyer, likewise, would have enjoyed good luck had he completed the purchase of the flock and sold at such a handsome profit.

"We did pursue this discussion to find a means by which good luck could be enticed to us. I feel that we have found the way. Both the tales did illustrate how good luck follows opportunity. Herein lies a truth that many similar tales of good luck, won or lost, could not change. The truth is this: *Good luck can be enticed by accepting opportunity.*

"Those eager to grasp opportunities for their betterment, do attract the interest of the good goddess. She is ever anxious to aid those who please her. Men of action please her best.

"Action will lead thee forward to the successes thou dost desire."

"A bag heavy with gold or a clay tablet carved with words of wisdom; if thou hadst thy choice, which wouldst thou choose?"

By the flickering light from the fire of desert shrubs, the sun-tanned faces of the listeners gleamed with interest.

"The gold, the gold," chorused the twenty-seven.

Old Kalabab smiled knowingly.

"Hark," he resumed, raising his hand. "Hear the wild dogs out there in the night. They howl and wail because they are lean with hunger. Yet feed them, and what do they? Fight and strut. Then fight and strut some more, giving no thought to the morrow that will surely come.

"Just so it is with the sons of men. Give them a choice of gold and wisdom—what do they do? Ignore the wisdom and waste the gold. On the morrow they wail because they have no more gold.

"Gold is reserved for those who know its laws and abide by them."

Kalabab drew his white robe close about his lean legs, for a cool night wind was blowing.

"Because thou hast served me faithfully upon our long journey, because thou cared well for my camels, because thou toiled uncomplainingly across the hot sands of the desert, because thou fought bravely the robbers that sought to despoil my merchandise, I will tell thee this night the tale of the five laws of gold, such a tale as thou never hast heard before.

"Hark ye, with deep attention to the words I speak, for if you grasp their meaning and heed them, in the days that come thou shalt have much gold."

He paused impressively. Above in a canopy of blue, the stars shone brightly in the crystal clear skies of Babylonia. Behind the group loomed their faded tents tightly staked against possible desert storms. Beside the tents were neatly stacked bales of merchandise covered with skins. Nearby the camel herd sprawled in the sand, some chewing their cuds contentedly, others snoring in hoarse discord.

"Thou hast told us many good tales, Kalabab," spoke up the chief packer. "We look to thy wisdom to guide us upon the morrow when our service with thee shall be at an end."

"I have but told thee of my adventures in strange and distant lands, but this night I shall tell thee of the wisdom of Arkad, the wise rich man."

"Much have we heard of him," acknowledged the chief packer, "for he was the richest man that ever lived in Babylon."

"The richest man he was, and that because he was wise in the ways of gold, even as no man had ever been before him. This night shall I tell you of his great wisdom as it was told to me by Nomasir, his son, many years ago in Nineveh, when I was but a lad.

"My master and myself had tarried long into the night in the palace of Nomasir. I had helped my master bring great bundles of fine rugs, each one to be tried by Nomasir until his choice of colors was satisfied. At last he was well pleased and commanded us to sit with him and to drink a rare vintage odorous to the nostrils and most warming to my stomach, which was unaccustomed to such a drink.

"Then, did he tell us this tale of the great wisdom of Arkad, his father, even as I shall tell it to you.

"In Babylon it is the custom, as you know, that the sons of wealthy fathers live with their parents in expectation of inheriting the estate. Arkad did not approve of this custom. Therefore, when Nomasir reached man's estate, he sent for the young man and addressed him:

" 'My son, it is my desire that thou succeed to my estate. Thou must, however, first prove that thou art capable of wisely handling it. Therefore, I wish that thou go out into the world and show thy ability both to acquire gold and to make thyself respected among men.

" 'To start thee well, I will give thee two things of which I, myself, was denied when I started as a poor youth to build up a fortune.

" 'First, I give thee this bag of gold. If thou use it wisely, it will be the basis of thy future success.

" 'Second, I give thee this clay tablet upon which is carved the five laws of gold. If thou dost but interpret them in thy own acts, they shall bring thee competence and security.

" 'Ten years from this day come thou back to the house of thy father and give account of thyself. If thou prove worthy, I will then make thee the heir to my estate. Otherwise, I will give it to the priests that they may barter for my soul the land consideration of the gods.'

"So Nomasir went forth to make his own way, taking his bag of gold, the clay tablet carefully wrapped in silken cloth, his slave and the horses upon which they rode.

"The ten years passed, and Nomasir, as he had agreed, returned to the house of his father who provided a great feast in his honor, to which he invited many friends and relatives. After the feast was over, the father and mother mounted their throne like seats at one side of the great hall, and Nomasir stood before them to give an account of himself as he had promised his father.

"It was evening. The room was hazy with smoke from the wicks of the oil lamps that but dimly lighted it. Slaves in white woven jackets and tunics fanned the humid air rhythmically with long-stemmed palm leaves. A stately dignity colored the scene. The wife of Nomasir and his two young sons, with friends and other members of the family, sat upon rugs behind him, eager listeners.

" 'My father,' he began deferentially, 'I bow before thy wisdom. Ten years ago when I stood at the gates of manhood, thou bade me go forth and become a man among men, instead of remaining a vassal to thy fortune.

" 'Thou gave me liberally of thy gold. Thou gave me liberally of thy wisdom. Of the gold, alas! I must admit of a disastrous handling. It fled, indeed, from my inexperienced hands even as a wild hare flees at the first opportunity from the youth who captures it.'

"The father smiled indulgently. 'Continue, my son, thy tale interests me in all its details.'

" 'I decided to go to Nineveh, as it was a growing city, believing that I might find there opportunities. I joined a caravan and among its members made numerous friends. Two well-spoken men who had a most beautiful white horse as fleet as the wind were among these.

" 'As we journeyed, they told me in confidence that in Nineveh was a wealthy man who owned a horse so swift that it had never been beaten. Its owner believed that no horse living could run with greater speed. Therefore, would he wager any sum however large that his horse could outspeed any horse in all Babylonia. Compared to their horse, so my friends said, it was but a lumbering ass that could be beaten with ease.

" 'They offered, as a great favor, to permit me to join them in a wager. I was quite carried away with the plan.

" 'Our horse was badly beaten and I lost much of my gold.' The father laughed. 'Later, I discovered that this was a deceitful plan of these men and they constantly journeyed with caravans seeking victims. You see, the man in Nineveh was their partner and shared with them the bets he won. This shrewd deceit taught me my first lesson in looking out for myself.

" 'I was soon to learn another, equally bitter. In the caravan was another young man with whom I became quite friendly. He was the son of wealthy parents and, like myself, journeying to Nineveh to find a suitable location. Not long after our arrival, he told me that a merchant had died and his shop with its rich merchandise and patronage could be secured at a paltry price. Saying that we would be equal partners but first he must return to Babylon to secure his gold, he prevailed upon me to purchase the stock with my gold, agreeing that his would be used later to carry on our venture.

“ ‘He long delayed the trip to Babylon, proving in the meantime to be an unwise buyer and a foolish spender. I finally put him out, but not before the business had deteriorated to where we had only unsalable goods and no gold to buy other goods. I sacrificed what was left to an Israelite for a pitiful sum.

“ ‘Soon there followed, I tell you, my father, bitter days. I sought employment and found it not, for I was without trade or training that would enable me to earn. I sold my horses. I sold my slave. I sold my extra robes that I might have food and a place to sleep, but each day grim want crouched closer.

“ ‘But in those bitter days, I remembered thy confidence in me, my father. Thou hadst sent me forth to become a man, and this I was determined to accomplish.’ The mother buried her face and wept softly.

“ ‘At this time, I bethought me of the table thou had given to me upon which thou had carved the five laws of gold. Thereupon, I read most carefully thy words of wisdom, and realized that had I but sought wisdom first, my gold would not have been lost to me. I learned by heart each law and determined that, when once more the goddess of good fortune smiled upon me, I would be guided by the wisdom of age and not by the inexperience of youth.

“ ‘For the benefit of you who are seated here this night, I will read the wisdom of my father as engraved upon the clay tablet which he gave to me ten years ago:

THE FIVE LAWS OF GOLD

I. Gold cometh gladly and in increasing quantity to any man who will put by not less than one-tenth of his earnings to create an estate for his future and that of his family.
II. Gold laboreth diligently and contentedly for the wise owner who finds for it profitable employment, multiplying even as the flocks of the field.
III. Gold clingeth to the protection of the cautious owner who invests it under the advice of men wise in its handling.
IV. Gold slippeth away from the man who invests it in businesses or purposes with which he is not familiar or which are not approved by those skilled in its keep.
V. Gold flees the man who would force it to impossible earnings or who followeth the alluring advice of tricksters and schemers or who trusts it to his own inexperience and romantic desires in investment.

“ ‘These are the five laws of gold as written by my father. I do proclaim them as of greater value than gold itself, as I will show by the continuance of my tale.’

“He again faced his father. ‘I have told thee of the depth of poverty and despair to which my inexperience brought me.

“ ‘However, there is no chain of disasters that will not come to an end. Mine came when I secured employment managing a crew of slaves working upon the new outer wall of the city.

“ ‘Profiting from my knowledge of the first law of gold, I saved a copper from my first earnings, adding to it at every opportunity until I had a piece of silver. It was a slow procedure, for one must live. I did spend grudgingly, I admit, because I was determined to earn back before the ten years were over as much gold as you, my father, had given to me.

“ ‘One day the slave master, with whom I had become quite friendly, said to me: “Thou art a thrifty youth who spends not wantonly what he earns. Hast thou gold put by that is not earning?”

“ ‘ “Yes,” I replied, “It is my greatest desire to accumulate gold to replace that which my father gave to me and which I have lost.”

“ ‘ “ ‘Tis a worthy ambition, I will grant, and do you know that the gold which you have saved can work for you and earn much more gold?”

“ ‘ “Alas! My experience has been bitter, for my father’s gold has fled from me, and I am in much fear lest my own do the same.”

“ ‘ “If thou hast confidence in me, I will give thee a lesson in the profitable handling of gold,” he replied. “Within a year the outer wall will be complete and ready for the great gates of bronze that will be built at each entrance to protect the city from the king’s enemies. In all Nineveh there is not enough metal to make these gates and the king has not thought to provide it. Here is my plan: A group of us will pool our gold and send a caravan to the mines of copper and tin, which are distant, and bring to Nineveh the metal for the gates. When the king says, ‘Make the great gates,’ we alone can supply the metal and a rich price he will pay. If the king will not buy from us, we will yet have the metal which can be sold for a fair price.”

“ ‘In his offer I recognized an opportunity to abide by the third law and invest my savings under the guidance of wise men. Nor was I disappointed. Our pool was a success, and my small store of gold was greatly increased by the transaction.

“ ‘In due time, I was accepted as a member of this same group in other ventures. They were men wise in the profitable handling of gold. They talked over each plan presented with great care, before entering upon it. They would take no chance on losing their principal or tying it up in unprofitable investments from which their gold could not be recovered. Such foolish things as the horse race and the partnership into which I had entered with my inexperience would have had scant consideration with them. They would have immediately pointed out their weaknesses.

" 'Through my association with these men, I learned to safely invest gold to bring profitable returns. As the years went on, my treasure increased more and more rapidly. I not only made back as much as I lost, but much more.

" 'Through my misfortunes, my trials and my success, I have tested time and again the wisdom of the five laws of gold, my father, and have proven them true in every test. To him who is without knowledge of the five laws, gold comes not often, and goeth away quickly. But to him who abide by the five laws, gold comes and works as his dutiful slave.'

"Nomasir ceased speaking and motioned to a slave in the back of the room. The slave brought forward, one at a time, three heavy leather bags. One of these Nomasir took and placed upon the floor before his father addressing him again:

" 'Thou didst give to me a bag of gold, Babylon gold. Behold in its place, I do return to thee a bag of Nineveh gold of equal weight An equal exchange, as all will agree.

" 'Thou didst give to me a clay tablet inscribed with wisdom. Behold, in its stead, I do return two bags of gold.' So saying, he took from the slave the other two bags and, likewise, placed them upon the floor before his father.

" 'This I do to prove to thee, my father, of how much greater value I consider thy wisdom than thy gold. Yet, who can measure in bags of gold, the value of wisdom? Without wisdom, gold is quickly lost by those who have it, but with wisdom, gold can be secured by those who have it not, as these three bags of gold do prove.

" 'It does, indeed, give to me the deepest satisfaction, my father, to stand before thee and say that, because of thy wisdom, I have been able to become rich and respected before men.'

"The father placed his hand fondly upon the head of Nomasir. 'Thou hast learned well thy lessons, and I am, indeed, fortunate to have a son to whom I may entrust my wealth.' "

Kalabab ceased his tale and looked critically at his listeners.

"What means this to thee, this tale of Nomasir?" he continued.

"Who amongst thee can go to thy father or to the father of thy wife and give an account of wise handling of his earnings?

"What would these venerable men think were you to say: 'I have traveled much and learned much and labored much and earned much, yet alas, of gold I have little. Some I spent wisely, some I spent foolishly and much I lost in unwise ways.'

"Dost still think it but an inconsistency of fate that some men have much gold and others have naught? Then you err.

"Men have much gold when they know the five laws of gold and abide thereby.

"Because I learned these five laws in my youth and abided by them, I have become a wealthy merchant. Not by some strange magic did I accumulate my wealth.

"Wealth that comes quickly goeth the same way.

"Wealth that stayeth to give enjoyment and satisfaction to its owner comes gradually, because it is a child born of knowledge and persistent purpose.

"To earn wealth is but a slight burden upon the thoughtful man. Bearing the burden consistently from year to year accomplishes the final purpose.

"The five laws of gold offer to thee a rich reward for their observance.

"Each of these five laws is rich with meaning and lest thou overlook this in the briefness of my tale, I will now repeat them. I do know them each by heart because in my youth, I could see their value and would not be content until I knew them word for word.

First Law of Gold: ***Gold cometh gladly and in increasing quantity to any man who will put by not less than one-tenth of his earnings to create an estate for his future and that of his family***.

"Any man who will put by one-tenth of his earnings consistently and invest it wisely will surely create a valuable estate that will provide an income for him in the future and further guarantee safety for his family in case the gods call him to the world of darkness. This law always sayeth that gold cometh gladly to such a man. I can truly certify this in my own life. The more gold I accumulate, the more readily it comes to me and in increased quantities. The gold which I save earns more, even as yours will, and its earnings earn more, and this is the working out of the first law."

Second Law of Gold: ***Gold laboreth diligently and contentedly for the wise owner who finds for it profitable employment, multiplying even as the flocks of the field.***

"Gold, indeed, is a willing worker. It is ever eager to multiply when opportunity presents itself. To every man who hath a store of gold set by, opportunity comes for its most profitable use. As the years pass, it multiplies itself in surprising fashion."

Third Law of Gold: ***Gold clingeth to the protection of the cautious owner who invests it under the advice of men wise in its handling.***

"Gold, indeed, clingeth to the cautious owner, even as it flees the careless owner. The man who seeks the advice of men wise in handling gold soon learneth not to jeopardize his treasure, but to preserve in safety and to enjoy in contentment its consistent increase."

Fourth Law of Gold: ***Gold slippeth away from the man who invests it in businesses or purposes with which he is not familiar or which are not approved by those skilled in its keep.***

"To the man who hath gold, yet is not skilled in its handling, many uses for it appear most profitable. Too often these are fraught with danger of loss, and if properly analyzed by wise men, show small possibility of profit. Therefore, the inexperienced owner of gold who trusts to his own judgment and invests it in business or purposes with which he is not familiar, too often finds his judgment imperfect, and pays with his treasure for his inexperience. Wise, indeed is he who investeth his treasures under the advice of men skilled in the ways of gold."

Fifth Law of Gold: ***Gold flees the man who would force it to impossible earnings or who followeth the alluring advice of tricksters and schemers or who trusts it to his own inexperience and romantic desires in investment.***

"Fanciful propositions that thrill like adventure tales always come to the new owner of gold. These appear to endow his treasure with magic powers that will enable it to make impossible earnings. Yet heed ye the wise men for verily they know the risks that lurk behind every plan to make great wealth suddenly.

"Forget not the rich men of Nineveh who would take no chance of losing their principal or tying it up in unprofitable investments.

"This ends my tale of the five laws of gold. In telling it to thee, I have told the secrets of my own success.

"Yet, they are not secrets but truths which every man must first learn and then follow who wishes to step out of the multitude that, like you wild dogs, must worry each day for food to eat.

"Tomorrow, we enter Babylon. Look! See the fire that burns eternal above the Temple of Bel! We are already in sight of the golden city. Tomorrow, each of thee shall have gold, the gold thou has so well earned by thy faithful services.

"Ten years from this night, what can you tell about this gold?

"If there be men among you, who, like Nomasir, will use a portion of their gold to start for themselves an estate and be thenceforth wisely guided by the wisdom of Arkad, ten years from now, 'tis a safe wager, like the son of Arkad, they will be rich and respected among men.

"Our wise acts accompany us through life to please us and to help us. Just as surely, our unwise acts follow us to plague and torment us. Alas, they cannot be forgotten. In the front rank of the torments that do follow us are the memories of the things we should have done, of the opportunities which came to us and we took not.

"Rich are the treasures of Babylon, so rich no man can count their value in pieces of gold. Each year, they grow richer and more valuable. Like the treasures of every land, they are a reward, a rich reward awaiting those men of purpose who determine to secure their just share.

"In the strength of thine own desires is a magic power. Guide this power with thy knowledge of the five laws of gold and thou shall share the treasures of Babylon."

PEOPLE OF ACTION ARE FAVORED

BY THE GODDESS OF GOOD LUCK.

6. The Gold Lender of Babylon

Fifty pieces of gold! Never before had Rodan, the spearmaker of old Babylon, carried so much gold in his leather wallet. Happily down the king's highway from the palace of his most liberal Majesty he strode. Cheerfully the gold clinked as the wallet at his belt swayed with each step—the sweetest music he had ever heard.

Fifty pieces of gold! All his! He could hardly realize his good fortune. What power in those clinking discs! They could purchase anything he wanted, a grand house, land, cattle, camels, horses, chariots, whatever he might desire.

What use should he make of it? This evening as he turned into a side street towards the home of his sister, he could think of nothing he would rather possess than those same glittering, heavy pieces of gold—his to keep.

It was upon an evening some days later that a perplexed Rodan entered the shop of Mathon, the lender of gold and dealer in jewels and rare fabrics. Glancing neither to the right nor the left at the colorful articles artfully displayed, he passed through to the living quarters at the rear. Here he found the genteel Mathon lounging upon a rug partaking of a meal served by a black slave.

"I would counsel with thee for I know not what to do." Rodan stood stolidly, feet apart, hairy breast exposed by the gaping front of his leather jacket.

Mathon's narrow, sallow face smiled a friendly greeting. "What indiscretions hast thou done that thou shouldst seek the lender of gold? Hast been unlucky at the gaming table? Or hath some plump dame entangled thee? For many years have I known thee, yet never hast thou sought me to aid thee in thy troubles."

"No, no. Not such as that. I seek no gold. Instead I crave thy wise advice."

"Hear! Hear! What this man doth say. No one comes to the lender of gold for advice. My ears must play me false."

"They listen true."

"Can this be so? Rodan, the spearmaker, doth display more cunning than all the rest, for he comes to Mathon, not for gold, but for advice. Many men come to me for gold to pay for their follies, but as for advice, they want it not. Yet who is more able to advice than the lender of gold to whom many men come in trouble?

"Thou shalt eat with me, Rodan," he continued. "Thou shalt be my guest for the evening. Andol!" he commanded of the black slave, "draw up a rag for my friend, Rodan, the spearmaker, who comes for advice. He shall be mine honored guest. Bring to him much food and get for him my largest cup. Choose well of the best wine that he may have satisfaction in the drinking.

"Now, tell me what troubles thee."

"It is the king's gift."

"The king's gift? The king did make thee a gift and it gives thee trouble? What manner of gift?"

"Because he was much pleased with the design I did submit to him for a new point on the spears of the royal guard, he did present me with fifty pieces of gold, and now I am much perplexed.

"I am beseeched each hour the sun doth travel across the sky by those who would share it with me."

"That is natural. More men want gold than have it, and would wish one who comes by it easily to divide. But can you not say 'No?' Is thy will not as strong as thy fist?"

"To many I can say no, yet sometimes it would be easier to say yes. Can one refuse to share with one's sister to whom he is deeply devoted?"

"Surely, thy own sister would not wish to deprive thee of enjoying thy reward."

"But it is for the sake of Araman, her husband, whom she wishes to see a rich merchant. She does feel that he has never had a chance and she beseeches me to loan to him this gold that he may become a prosperous merchant and repay me from his profits."

"My friend," resumed Mathon, " 'tis a worthy subject thou bringest to discuss. Gold bringeth unto its possessor responsibility and a changed position with his fellow men. It bringeth fear lest he lose it or it be tricked away from him. It bringeth a feeling of power and ability to do good. Likewise, it bringeth opportunities whereby his very good intentions may bring him into difficulties.

"Didst ever hear of the farmer of Nineveh who could understand the language of animals? I wot not, for 'tis not the kind of tale men like to tell over the bronze caster's forge. I will tell it to thee for thou shouldst know that to borrowing and lending there is more than the passing of gold from the hands of one to the hands of another.

"This farmer, who could understand what the animals said to each other, did linger in the farm yard each evening just to listen to their words. One evening he did hear the ox bemoaning to the ass the hardness of his lot: 'I do labor pulling the plow from morning until night. No matter how hot the day, or how tired my legs, or how the bow doth chafe my neck, still must I work. But you are a creature of leisure. You are trapped with a colorful blanket and do nothing more than carry our master about where he wishes to go. When he goes nowhere you do rest and eat the green grass all the day.'

"Now the ass, in spite of his vicious heels, was a goodly fellow and sympathized with the ox. 'My good friend,' he replied, 'you do work very hard and I would help ease your lot. Therefore, will I tell you how you may have a day of rest. In the morning when the slave comes to fetch you to the plow, lie upon the ground and bellow much that he may say you are sick and cannot work.'

"So the ox took the advice of the ass and the next morning the slave returned to the farmer and told him the ox was sick and could not pull the plow.

" 'Then,' said the farmer, 'hitch the ass to the plow for the plowing must go on.'

"All that day the ass, who had only intended to help his friend, found himself compelled to do the ox's task. When night came and he was released from the plow his heart was bitter and his legs were weary and his neck was sore where the bow had chafed it.

"The farmer lingered in the barnyard to listen.

"The ox began first. 'You are my good friend. Because of your wise advice I have enjoyed a day of rest.'

" 'And I,' retorted the ass, 'am like many another simple hearted one who starts to help a friend and ends up by doing his task for him. Hereafter you draw your own plow, for I did hear the master tell the slave to send for the butcher were you sick again. I wish he would, for you are a lazy fellow.' Thereafter they spoke to each other no more— this ended their friendship. Canst thou tell the moral to this tale, Rodan?"

" 'Tis a good tale," responded Rodan, "but I see not the moral."

"I thought not that you would. But it is there and simple too. Just this: If you desire to help thy friend, do so in a way that will not bring thy friend's burdens upon thyself."

"I had not thought of that. It is a wise moral. I wish not to assume the burdens of my sister's husband. But tell me. You lend too many. Do not the borrowers repay?"

Mathon smiled the smile of one whose soul is rich with much experience. "Could a loan be well made if the borrower cannot repay? Must not the lender be wise and judge carefully whether his gold can perform a useful purpose to the borrower and return to him once more; or whether it will be wasted by one unable to use it wisely and leave him without his treasure, and leave the borrower with a debt he cannot repay? I will show to thee the tokens in my token chest and let them tell thee some of their stories."

Into the room he brought a chest as long as his arm covered with red pigskin and ornamented with bronze designs. He placed it upon the floor and squatted before it, both hands upon the lid.

"From each person to whom I lend, I do exact a token for my token chest, to remain there until the loan is repaid. When they repay I give back, but if they never repay it will always remind me of one who was not faithful to my confidence.

"The safest loans, my token box tells me, are to those whose possessions are of more value than the one they desire. They own lands, or jewels, or camels, or other things which could be sold to repay the loan. Some of the tokens given to me are jewels of more value than the loan. Others are promises that if the loan be not repaid as agreed they will deliver to me certain property settlement. On loans like those I am assured that my gold will be returned with the rental thereon, for the loan is based on property.

"In another class are those who have the capacity to earn. They are such as you, who labor or serve and are paid. They have income and if they are honest and suffer no misfortune, I know that they also can repay the gold I loan them and the rental to which I am entitled. Such loans are based on human effort.

"Others are those who have neither property nor assured earning capacity. Life is hard and there will always be some who cannot adjust themselves to it. Alas for the loans I make them, even though they be no larger than a pence, my token box may censure me in the years to come unless they be guaranteed by good friends of the borrower who know him honorable."

Mathon released the clasp and opened the lid. Rodan leaned forward eagerly.

At the top of the chest a bronze neck-piece lay upon a scarlet cloth. Mathon picked up the piece and patted it affectionately. "This shall always remain in my token chest because the owner has passed on into the great darkness. I treasure it, his token, and I treasure his memory; for he was my good friend. We traded together with much success until out of the east he brought a woman to wed, beautiful, but not like our women. A dazzling creature. He spent his gold lavishly to gratify her desires. He came to me in distress when his gold was gone. I counseled with him. I told him I would help him to once more master his own affairs. He swore by the sign of the Great Bull that he would. But it was not to be. In a quarrel she thrust a knife into the heart he dared her to pierce."

"And she?" questioned Rodan.

"Yes, of course, this was hers." He picked up the scarlet cloth. "In bitter remorse she threw herself into the Euphrates. These two loans will never be repaid. The chest tells you, Rodan, that humans in the throes of great emotions are not safe risks for the gold lender.

"Here! Now this is different." He reached for a ring carved of ox bone. "This belongs to a farmer. I buy the rugs of his women. The locusts came and they had not food. I helped him and when the new crop came he repaid me. Later he came again and told of strange goats in a distant land as described by a traveler. They had long hair so fine and soft it would weave into rugs more beautiful than any ever seen in Babylon. He wanted a herd but he had no money. So I did lend him gold to make the journey and bring back goats. Now his herd is begun and next year I shall surprise the lords of Babylon with the most expensive rugs it has been their good fortune to buy. Soon I must return his ring. He doth insist on repaying promptly."

"Some borrowers do that?" queried Rodan.

"If they borrow for purposes that bring money back to them, I find it so. But if they borrow because of their indiscretions, I warn thee to be cautious if thou wouldst ever have thy gold back in hand again."

"Tell me about this," requested Rodan, picking up a heavy gold bracelet inset with jewels in rare designs.

"The women do appeal to my good friend," bantered Mathon.

"I am still much younger than you," retorted Rodan.

"I grant that, but this time thou doth suspicion romance where it is not. The owner of this is fat and wrinkled and doth talk so much and say so little she drives me mad. Once they had much money and were good customers, but ill times came upon them. She has a son of whom she would make a merchant. So she came to me and borrowed gold that he might become a partner of a caravan owner who travels with his camels bartering in one city what he buys in another.

"This man proved a rascal for he left the poor boy in a distant city without money and without friends, pulling out early while the youth slept. Perhaps when this youth has grown to manhood, he will repay; until then I get no rental for the loan—only much talk. But I do admit the jewels are worthy of the loan."

"Did this lady ask thy advice as to the wisdom of the loan?"

"Quite otherwise. She had pictured to herself this son of hers as a wealthy and powerful man of Babylon. To suggest the contrary was to infuriate her. A fair rebuke I had. I knew the risk for this inexperienced boy, but as she offered security I could not refuse her.

"This," continued Mathon, waving a bit of pack rope tied into a knot, "belongs to Nebatur, the camel trader. When he would buy a herd larger than his funds he brings to me this knot and I lend to him according to his needs. He is a wise trader. I have confidence in his good judgment and can lend him freely. Many other merchants of Babylon have my confidence because of their honorable behavior. Their tokens come and go frequently in my token box. Good merchants are an asset to our city and it profits me to aid them to keep trade moving that Babylon be prosperous."

Mathon picked out a beetle carved in turquoise and tossed it contemptuously on the floor. "A bug from Egypt. The lad who owns this does not care whether I ever receive back my gold. When I reproach him he replies, 'How can I repay when ill fate pursues me? You have plenty more.' What can I do? The token is his father's—a worthy man of small means who did pledge his land and herd to back his son's enterprises. The youth found success at first and then was over-zealous to gain great wealth. His knowledge was immature. His enterprises collapsed. "Youth is ambitious. Youth would take short cuts to wealth and the desirable things for which it stands. To secure wealth quickly youth often borrows unwisely.

"Youth, never having had experience, cannot realize that hopeless debt is like a deep pit into which one may descend quickly and where one may struggle vainly for many days. It is a pit of sorrow and regrets where the brightness of the sun is overcast and night is made unhappy by restless sleeping. Yet, I do not discourage borrowing gold. I encourage it. I recommend it if it be for a wise purpose. I myself made my first real success as a merchant with borrowed gold.

"Yet, what should the lender do in such a case? The youth is in despair and accomplishes nothing. He is discouraged. He makes no effort to repay. My heart turns against depriving the father of his land and cattle."

"You tell me much that I am interested to hear," ventured Rodan, "but, I hear no answer to my question. Should I lend my fifty pieces of gold to my sister's husband? They mean much to me."

"Thy sister is a sterling woman whom I do much esteem. Should her husband come to me and ask to borrow fifty pieces of gold I should ask him for what purpose he would use it.

"If he answered that he desired to become a merchant like myself and deal in jewels and rich furnishings. I would say, 'What knowledge have you of the ways of trade? Do you know where you can buy at lowest cost? Do you know where you can sell at a fair price?' Could he say 'Yes' to these questions?"

"No, he could not," Rodan admitted. "He has helped me much in making spears and he has helped some in the shops."

"Then, would I say to him that his purpose was not wise. Merchants must learn their trade. His ambition, though worthy, is not practical and I would not lend him any gold.

"But, supposing he could say: 'Yes, I have helped merchants much. I know how to travel to Smyrna and to buy at low cost the rugs the housewives weave. I also know many of the rich people of Babylon to whom I can sell these at a large profit.' Then I would say: 'Your purpose is wise and your ambition honorable. I shall be glad to lend you the fifty pieces of gold if you can give me security that they will be returned." But would he say, 'I have no security other than that I am an honored man and will pay you well for the loan.' Then would I reply, 'I treasure much each piece of gold. Were the robbers to take it from you as you journeyed to Smyrna or take the rugs from you as you returned, then you would have no means of repaying me and my gold would be gone.'

"Gold, you see, Rodan, is the merchandise of the lender of money. It is easy to lend. If it is lent unwisely then it is difficult to get back. The wise lender wishes not the risk of the undertaking but the guarantee of safe repayment.

" 'Tis well," he continued, "to assist those that are in trouble, 'tis well to help those upon whom fate has laid a heavy hand. 'Tis well to help those who are starting that they may progress and become valuable citizens. But help must be given wisely, lest, like the farmer's ass, in our desire to help we but take upon ourselves the burden that belongs to another.

"Again I wandered from thy question, Rodan, but hear my answer: Keep thy fifty pieces of gold. What thy labor earns for thee and what is given thee for reward is thine own and no man can put an obligation upon thee to part with it unless it do be thy wish. If thee wouldst lend it so that it may earn thee more gold, then lend with caution and in many places. I like not idle gold, even less I like too much of risk.

"How many years hast thou labored as a spearmaker?"

"Fully three."

"How much besides the King's gift hast saved?"

"Three gold pieces."

"Each year that thou hast labored thou has denied thyself good things to save from thine earnings one piece of gold?"

" 'Tis as you say."

"Then mightest save in fifty years of labor fifty pieces of gold by thy self-denial?"

"A lifetime of labor it would be."

"Thinkest thou thy sister would wish to jeopardize the savings of fifty years of labor over the bronze melting pot that her husband might experiment on being a merchant?"

"Not if I spoke in your words."

"Then go to her and say: 'Three years I have labored each day except fast days, from morning until night, and I have denied myself many things that my heart craved. For each year of labor and self-denial I have to show one piece of gold. Thou art my favored sister and I wish that thy husband may engage in business in which he will prosper greatly. If he will submit to me a plan that seems wise and possible to my friend, Mathon, then will I gladly lend to him my savings of an entire year that he may have an opportunity to prove that he can succeed.' Do that, I say, and if he has within him the soul to succeed he can prove it. If he fails he will not owe thee more than he can hope someday to repay.

"I am a gold lender because I own more gold than I can use in my own trade. I desire my surplus gold to labor for others and thereby earn more gold. I do not wish to take risk of losing my gold for I have labored much and denied myself much to secure it. Therefore, I will no longer lend any of it where I am not confident that it is safe and will be returned to me. Neither will I lend it where I am not convinced that its earnings will be promptly paid to me.

"I have told to thee, Rodan, a few of the secrets of my token chest. From them you may understand the weakness of men and their eagerness to borrow that which they have no certain means to repay. From this you can see how often their high hopes of the great earnings they could make, if they but had gold, are but false hopes they have not the ability or training to fulfill.

"Thou, Rodan, now have gold which thou shouldst put to earning more gold for thee. Thou art about to become even as I, a gold lender. If thou dost safely preserve thy treasure it will produce liberal earnings for thee and be a rich source of pleasure and profit during all thy days. But if thou dost let it escape from thee, it will be a source of constant sorrow and regret as long as thy memory doth last.

"What desirest thou most of this gold in thy wallet?"

"To keep it safe."

"Wisely spoken," replied Mathon approvingly. "Thy first desire is for safety. Thinkest thou that in the custody of thy sister's husband it would be truly safe from possible loss?"

"I fear not, for he is not wise in guarding gold."

"Then be not swayed by foolish sentiments of obligation to trust thy treasure to any person. If thou wouldst help thy family or thy friends, find other ways than risking the loss of thy treasure. Forget not that gold slippeth away in unexpected ways from those unskilled in guarding it. As well waste thy treasure in extravagance as let others lose it for thee.

"What next after safety dost desire of this treasure of thine?"

"That it earn more gold."

"Again thou speakest with wisdom. It should be made to earn and grow larger. Gold wisely lent may even double itself with its earnings before a man like you groweth old. If you risk losing it you risk losing all that it would earn as well.

"Therefore, be not swayed by the fantastic plans of impractical men who think they see ways to force thy gold to make earnings unusually large. Such plans are the creations of dreamers unskilled in the safe and dependable laws of trade. Be conservative in what thou expect it to earn that thou mayest keep and enjoy thy treasure. To hire it out with a promise of usurious returns is to invite loss.

"Seek to associate thyself with men and enterprises whose success is established that thy treasure may earn liberally under their skillful use and be guarded safely by their wisdom and experience.

"Thus, mayest thou avoid the misfortunes that follow most of the sons of men to whom the gods see fit to entrust gold."

When Rodan would thank him for his wise advice he would not listen, saying, "The king's gift shall teach thee much wisdom. If wouldst keep thy fifty pieces of gold thou must be discreet indeed. Many uses will tempt thee. Much advice will be spoken to thee. Numerous opportunities to make large profits will be offered thee. The stories from my token box should warn thee, before thou let any piece of gold leave thy pouch to be sure that thou hast a safe way to pull it back again. Should my further advice appeal to thee, return again. It is gladly given.

" 'E're thou goest read this which I have carved beneath the lid of my token box. It applies equally to the borrower and the lender:

BETTER A LITTLE CAUTION
THAN A GREAT REGRET

7. The Walls of Babylon

Old Banzar, grim warrior of another day, stood guard at the passageway leading to the top of the ancient walls of Babylon. Up above, valiant defenders were battling to hold the walls. Upon them depended the future existence of this great city with its hundreds of thousands of citizens.

Over the walls came the roar of the attacking armies, the yelling of many men, the trampling of thousands of horses, the deafening boom of the battering rams pounding the bronzed gates.

In the street behind the gate lounged the spearmen, waiting to defend the entrance should the gates give way. They were but few for the task. The main armies of Babylon were with their king, far away in the east on the great expedition against the Elamites. No attack upon the city having been anticipated during their absence, the defending forces were small. Unexpectedly, from the north, bore down the mighty armies of the Assyrians. And now the walls must hold or Babylon was doomed.

About Banzar were great crowds of citizens, white-faced and terrified, eagerly seeking news of the battle. With hushed awe they viewed the stream of wounded and dead being carried or led out of the passageway.

Here was the crucial point of attack. After three days of circling about the city, the enemy had suddenly thrown his great strength against this section and this gate.

The defenders from the top of the wall fought off the climbing platforms and the scaling ladders of the attackers with arrows, burning oil and, if any reached the top, spears. Against the defenders, thousands of the enemy's archers poured a deadly barrage of arrows.

Old Banzar had the vantage point for news. He was closest to the conflict and first to hear of each fresh repulse of the frenzied attackers.

An elderly merchant crowded close to him, his palsied hands quivering. "Tell me! Tell me!" he pleaded. "They cannot get in. My sons are with the good king. There is no one to protect my old wife. My goods, they will steal all. My food, they will leave nothing. We are old, too old to defend ourselves —too old for slaves. We shall starve. We shall die. Tell me they cannot get in."

"Calm thyself, good merchant," the guard responded. "The walls of Babylon are strong. Go back to the bazaar and tell your wife that the walls will protect you and all of your possessions as safely as they protect the rich treasures of the king. Keep close to the walls, lest the arrows flying over strike you!"

A woman with a babe in arms took the old man's place as he withdrew. "Sergeant, what news from the top? Tell me truly that I may reassure my poor husband. He lies with fever from his terrible wounds, yet insists upon his armor and his spear to protect me, who am with child. Terrible he says will be the vengeful lust of our enemies should they break in."

"Be thou of good heart, thou mother that is, and is again to be, the walls of Babylon will protect you and your babes. They are high and strong. Hear ye not the yells of our valiant defenders as they empty the caldrons of burning oil upon the ladder scalers?"

"Yes, that do I hear and also the roar of the battering rams that do hammer at our gates."

"Back to thy husband. Tell him the gates are strong and withstand the rams. Also that the scalers climb the walls but to receive the waiting spear thrust. Watch, thy way and hasten behind you buildings."

Banzar stepped aside to clear the passage for heavily armed reinforcements. As, with clanking bronze shields and heavy tread, they tramped by, a small girl plucked at his girdle.

"Tell me please, soldier, are we safe?" she pleaded. "I hear the awful noises. I see the men all bleeding. I am so frightened. What will become of our family, of my mother, little brother and the baby?"

The grim old campaigner blinked his eyes and thrust forward his chin as he beheld the child.

"Be not afraid, little one," he reassured her. "The walls of Babylon will protect you and mother and little brother and the baby. It was for the safety of such as you that the good Queen Semiramis built them over a hundred years ago. Never have they been broken through. Go back and tell your mother and little brother and the baby that the walls of Babylon will protect them and they need have no fear."

Day after day old Banzar stood at his post and watched the reinforcements file up the passageway, there to stay and fight until wounded or dead they came down once more. Around him, unceasingly crowded the throngs of frightened citizens eagerly seeking to learn if the walls would hold. To all he gave his answer with the fine dignity of an old soldier, "The walls of Babylon will protect you."

For three weeks and five days the attack waged with scarcely ceasing violence. Harder and grimmer set the jaw of Banzar as the passage behind, wet with the blood of the many wounded, was churned into mud by the never ceasing streams of men passing up and staggering down. Each day the slaughtered attackers piled up in heaps before the wall. Each night they were carried back and buried by their comrades.

Upon the fifth night of the fourth week the clamor without diminished. The first streaks of daylight, illuminating the plains, disclosed great clouds of dust raised by the retreating armies.

A mighty shout went up from the defenders. There was no mistaking its meaning. It was repeated by the waiting troops behind the walls. It was echoed by the citizens upon the streets. It swept over the city with the violence of a storm.

People rushed from the houses. The streets were jammed with a throbbing mob. The pent-up fear of weeks found an outlet in the wild chorus of joy. From the top of the high tower of the Temple of Bel burst forth the flames of victory. Skyward floated the column of blue smoke to carry the message far and wide.

The walls of Babylon had once again repulsed a mighty and viscous foe determined to loot her rich treasures and to ravish and enslave her citizens.

Babylon endured century after century because it was *fully protected.* It could not afford to be otherwise.

The walls of Babylon were an outstanding example of man's need and desire for protection. This desire is inherent in the human race. It is just as strong today as it ever was, but we have developed broader and better plans to accomplish the same purpose.

In this day, behind the impregnable walls of insurance, savings accounts and dependable investments, we can guard ourselves against the unexpected tragedies that may enter any door and seat themselves before any fireside.

WE CANNOT AFFORD TO BE WITHOUT ADEQUATE PROTECTION

8. The Camel Trader of Babylon

The hungrier one becomes, the clearer one's mind works— also the more sensitive one becomes to the odors of food. Tarkad, the son of Azure, certainly thought so. For two whole days he had tasted no food except two small figs purloined from over the wall of a garden. Not another could he grab before the angry woman rushed forth and chased him down the street. Her shrill cries were still ringing in his ears as he walked through the market place. They helped him to retrain his restless fingers from snatching the tempting fruits from the baskets of the market women.

Never before had he realized how much food was brought to the markets of Babylon and how good it smelled. Leaving the market, he walked across to the inn and paced back and forth in front of the eating house. Perhaps here he might meet someone he knew; someone from whom he could borrow a copper that would gain him a smile from the unfriendly keeper of the inn and, with it, a liberal helping. Without the copper he knew all too well how unwelcome he would be.

In his abstraction he unexpectedly found himself face to face with the one man he wished most to avoid, the tall bony figure of Dabasir, the camel trader. Of all the friends and others from whom he had borrowed small sums, Dabasir made him feel the most uncomfortable because of his failure to keep his promises to repay promptly.

Dabasir's face lighted up at the sight of him. "Ha! 'Tis Tarkad, just the one I have been seeking that he might repay the two pieces of copper which I lent him a moon ago; also the piece of silver which I lent to him before that. We are well met. I can make good use of the coins this very day. What say, boy? What say?"

Tarkad stuttered and his face flushed. He had naught in his empty stomach to nerve him to argue with the outspoken Dabasir. "I am sorry, very sorry," he mumbled weakly, "but this day I have neither the copper nor the silver with which I could repay."

"Then get it," Dabasir insisted. "Surely thou canst get hold of a few coppers and a piece of silver to repay the generosity of an old friend of thy father who aided thee whenst thou wast in need?"

" 'Tis because ill fortune does pursue me that I cannot pay."

"Ill fortune! Wouldst blame the gods for thine own weakness. Ill fortune pursues every man who thinks more of borrowing than of repaying. Come with me, boy, while I eat. I am hungry and I would tell thee a tale."

Tarkad flinched from the brutal frankness of Dabasir, but here at least was an invitation to enter the coveted doorway of the eating house.

Dabasir pushed him to a far corner of the room where they seated themselves upon small rugs.

When Kauskor, the proprietor, appeared smiling, Dabasir addressed him with his usual freedom, "Fat lizard of the desert, bring to me a leg of the goat, brown with much juice, and bread and all of the vegetables for I am hungry and want much food. Do not forget my friend here. Bring to him a jug of water. Have it cooled, for the day is hot."

Tarkad's heart sank. Must he sit here and drink water while he watched this man devour an entire goat leg? He said nothing. He thought of nothing he could say.

Dabasir, however, knew no such thing as silence. Smiling and waving his hand good-naturedly to the other customers, all of whom knew him, he continued.

"I did hear from a traveler just returned from Urfa of a certain rich man who has a piece of stone cut so thin that one can look through it. He put it in the window of his house to keep out the rains. It is yellow, so this traveler does relate, and he was permitted to look through it and all the outside world looked strange and not like it really is. What say you to that, Tarkad? Thinkest all the world could look to a man a different color from what it is?"

"I dare say," responded the youth, much more interested in the fat leg of goat placed before Dabasir.

"Well, I know it to be true for I myself have seen the world all of a different color from what it really is and the tale I am about to tell relates how I came to see it in its right color once more."

"Dabasir will tell a tale," whispered a neighboring diner to his neighbor, and dragged his rug close. Other diners brought their food and crowded in a semi-circle. They crunched noisily in the ears of Tarkad and brushed him with their meaty bones. He alone was without food. Dabasir did not offer to share with him nor even motion him to a small corner of the hard bread that was broken off and had fallen from the platter to the floor.

"The tale that I am about to tell," began Dabasir, pausing to bite a goodly chunk from the goat leg, "relates to my early life and how I came to be a camel trader. Didst anyone know that I once was a slave in Syria?"

A murmur of surprise ran through the audience to which Dabasir listened with satisfaction.

"When I was a young man," continued Dabasir after another vicious onslaught on the goat leg, "I learned the trade of my father, the making of saddles. I worked with him in his shop and took to myself a wife. Being young and not greatly skilled, I could earn but little, just enough to support my excellent wife in a modest way. I craved good things which I could not afford. Soon I found that the shop keepers would trust me to pay later even though I could not pay at the time.

"Being young and without experience I did not know that he who spends more than he earns is sowing the winds of needless self-indulgence from which he is sure to reap the whirlwinds of trouble and humiliation. So I indulged my whims for fine raiment and bought luxuries for my good wife and our home, beyond our means.

"I paid as I could and for a while all went well. But in time I discovered I could not use my earnings both to live upon and to pay my debts. Creditors began to pursue me to pay for my extravagant purchases and my life became miserable. I borrowed from my friends, but could not repay them either. Things went from bad to worse. My wife returned to her father and I decided to leave Babylon and seek another city where a young man might have better chances.

"For two years I had a restless and unsuccessful life working for caravan traders. From this I fell in with a set of likeable robbers who scoured the desert for unarmed caravans. Such deeds were unworthy of the son of my father, but I was seeing the world through a colored stone and did not realize to what degradation I had fallen.

"We met with success on our first trip, capturing a rich haul of gold and silks and valuable merchandise. This loot we took to Ginir and squandered.

"The second time we were not so fortunate. Just after we had made our capture, we were attacked by the spearsmen of a native chief to whom the caravans paid for protection. Our two leaders were killed, and the rest of us were taken to Damascus where we were stripped of our clothing and sold as slaves.

"I was purchased for two pieces of silver by a Syrian desert chief. With my hair shorn and but a loin cloth to wear, I was not so different from the other slaves. Being a reckless youth, I thought it merely an adventure until my master took me before his four wives and told them they could have me for a eunuch.

"Then, indeed, did I realize the hopelessness of my situation. These men of the desert were fierce and warlike. I was subject to their will without weapons or means of escape.

"Fearful I stood, as those four women looked me over. I wondered if I could expect pity from them. Sira, the first wife, was older than the others. Her face was impassive as she looked upon me. I turned from her with little consolation. The next was a contemptuous beauty who gazed at me as indifferently as if I had been a worm of the earth. The two younger ones tittered as though it were all an exciting joke.

“It seemed an age that I stood waiting sentence. Each woman appeared willing for the others to decide. Finally Sira spoke up in a cold voice.

“ ‘Of eunuchs we have plenty, but of camel tenders we have few and they are a worthless lot. Even this day I would visit my mother who is sick with the fever and there is no slave I would trust to lead my camel. Ask this slave if he can lead a camel.’

“My master thereupon questioned me, ‘What know you of camels?’

“Striving to conceal my eagerness, I replied, ‘I can make them kneel, I can load them, I can lead them on long trips without tiring. If need be, I can repair their trappings.’

“ ‘The slave speaks forward enough,’ observed my master. ‘If thou so desire, Sira, take this man for thy camel tender.’

“So I was turned over to Sira and that day I led her camel upon a long journey to her sick mother. I took the occasion to thank her for her intercession and also to tell her that I was not a slave by birth, but the son of a free man, an honorable saddle maker of Babylon. I also told her much of my story. Her comments were disconcerting to me and I pondered much afterwards on what she said.

“ ‘How can you call yourself a free man when your weakness has brought you to this? If a man has in himself the soul of a slave, will he not become one no matter what his birth, even as water seeks its level? If a man has within him the soul of a free man, will he not become respected and honored in his own city in spite of his misfortune?’

“For over a year I was a slave and lived with the slaves, but I could not become as one of them. One day Sira asked me, ‘In the eventime when the other slaves can mingle and enjoy the society of each other, why dost thou sit in thy tent alone?’

“To which I responded, ‘I am pondering what you have said to me. I wonder if I have the soul of a slave. I cannot join them, so I must sit apart.’

“ ‘I, too, must sit apart,’ she confided. ‘My dowry was large and my lord married me because of it. Yet he does not desire me. What every woman longs for is to be desired. Because of this and because I am barren and have neither son nor daughter, must I sit apart. Were I a man I would rather die than be such a slave, but the conventions of our tribe make slaves of women.’

“ ‘What think thou of me by this time?’ I asked her suddenly, ‘Have I the soul of a man or have I the soul of a slave?’

“ ‘Have you a desire to repay the just debts you owe in Babylon?’ she parried.

" 'Yes, I have the desire, but I see no way.'

" If thou contentedly let the years slip by and make no effort to repay, then thou hast but the contemptible soul of a slave. No man is otherwise who cannot respect himself and no man can respect himself who does not repay honest debts.'

" 'But what can I do who am a slave in Syria?'

" 'Stay a slave in Syria, thou weakling.'

" 'I am not a weakling,' I denied hotly.

" 'Then prove it.'

" 'How?'

" 'Does not thy great king fight his enemies in every way he can and with every force he has? Thy debts are thy enemies. They ran thee out of Babylon. You left them alone and they grew too strong for thee. Hadst fought them as a man, thou couldst have conquered them and been one honored among the townspeople. But thou had not the soul to fight them and behold thy pride hast gone down until thou art a slave in Syria.'

"Much I thought over her unkind accusations and many defensive phrases I worded to prove myself not a slave at heart, but I was not to have the chance to use them. Three days later the maid of Sira took me to her mistress.

" 'My mother is again very sick,' she said. 'Saddle the two best camels in my husband's herd. Tie on water skins and saddle bags for a long journey. The maid will give thee food at the kitchen tent.' I packed the camels wondering much at the quantity of provisions the maid provided, for the mother dwelt less than a day's journey away. The maid rode the rear camel which followed and I led the camel of my mistress. When we reached her mother's house it was just dark. Sira dismissed the maid and said to me:

" 'Dabasir, hast thou the soul of a free man or the soul of a slave?'

" 'The soul of a free man,' I insisted.

" 'Now is thy chance to prove it. Thy master hath imbibed deeply and his chiefs are in a stupor. Take then these camels and make thy escape. Here in this bag is raiment of thy master's to disguise thee. I will say thou stole the camels and ran away while I visited my sick mother.'

" 'Thou hast the soul of a queen,' I told her. 'Much do I wish that I might lead thee to happiness.'

" 'Happiness,' she responded, 'awaits not the runaway wife who seeks it in far lands among strange people. Go thy own way and may the gods of the desert protect thee for the way is far and barren of food or water.'

"I needed no further urging, but thanked her warmly and was away into the night. I knew not this strange country and had only a dim idea of the direction in which lay Babylon, but struck out bravely across the desert toward the hills. One camel I rode and the other I led. All that night I traveled and all the next day, urged on by the knowledge of the terrible fate that was meted out to slaves who stole their master's property and tried to escape.

"Late that afternoon, I reached a rough country as uninhabitable as the desert. The sharp rocks bruised the feet of my faithful camels and soon they were picking their way slowly and painfully along. I met neither man nor beast and could well understand why they shunned this inhospitable land.

"It was such a journey from then on as few men live to tell of. Day after day we plodded along. Food and water gave out. The heat of the sun was merciless. At the end of the ninth day, I slid from the back of my mount with the feeling that I was too weak to ever remount and I would surely die, lost in this abandoned country.

"I stretched out upon the ground and slept, not waking until the first gleam of daylight.

"I sat up and looked about me. There was a coolness in the morning air. My camels lay dejected not far away. About me was a vast waste of broken country covered with rock and sand and thorny things, no sign of water, naught to eat for man or camel.

"Could it be that in this peaceful quiet I faced my end? My mind was clearer than it had ever been before. My body now seemed of little importance. My parched and bleeding lips, my dry and swollen tongue, my empty stomach, all had lost their supreme agonies of the day before.

"I looked across into the uninviting distance and once again came to me the question, 'Have I the soul of a slave or the soul of a free man?' Then with clearness I realized that if I had the soul of a slave, I should give up, lie down in the desert and die, a fitting end for a runaway slave.

"But if I had the soul of a free man, what then? Surely I would force my way back to Babylon, repay the people who had trusted me, bring happiness to my wife who truly loved me and bring peace and contentment to my parents.

" 'Thy debts are thine enemies who have run thee out of Babylon,' Sira had said. Yes it was so. Why had I refused to stand my ground like a man? Why had I permitted my wife to go back to her father?

"Then a strange thing happened. All the world seemed to be of a different color as though I had been looking at it through a colored stone which had suddenly been removed. At last I saw the true values in life.

"Die in the desert! Not I! With a new vision, I saw the things that I must do. First I would go back to Babylon and face every man to whom I owed an unpaid debt. I should tell them that after years of wandering and misfortune, I had come back to pay my debts as fast as the gods would permit. Next I should make a home for my wife and become a citizen of whom my parents should be proud.

"My debts were my enemies, but the men I owed were my friends for they had trusted me and believed in me.

"I staggered weakly to my feet. What mattered hunger? What mattered thirst? They were but incidents on the road to Babylon. Within me surged the soul of a free man going back to conquer his enemies and reward his friends. I thrilled with the great resolve.

"The glazed eyes of my camels brightened at the new note in my husky voice. With great effort, after many attempts, they gained their feet. With pitiful perseverance, they pushed on toward the north where something within me said we would find Babylon.

"We found water. We passed into a more fertile country where grass and fruit were. We found the trail to Babylon because the soul of a free man looks at life as a series of problems to be solved and solves them, while the soul of a slave whines, 'What can I do who am but a slave?'

"How about thee, Tarkad? Dost thy empty stomach make thy head exceedingly clear? Art ready to take the road that leads back to self respect? Canst thou see the world in its true color? Hast thou the desire to pay thy honest debts, however many they may be, and once again be a man respected in Babylon?"

Moisture came to the eyes of the youth. He rose eagerly to his knees. "Thou has shown me a vision; already I feel the soul of a free man surge within me."

"But how fared you upon your return?" questioned an interested listener.

"Where the determination is, the way can be found" Dabasir replied. "I now had the determination so I set out to find a way. First I visited every man to whom I was indebted and begged his indulgence until I could earn that with which to repay. Most of them met me gladly. Several reviled me but others offered to help me; one indeed did give me the very help I needed. It was Mathon, the gold lender. Learning that I had been a camel tender in Syria; he sent me to old Nebatur, the camel trader, just

commissioned by our good king to purchase many herds of sound camels for the great expedition. With him, my knowledge of camels I put to good use. Gradually I was able to repay every copper and every piece of silver. Then at last I could hold up my head and feel that I was an honorable man among men."

Again Dabasir turned to his food. "Kauskor, thou snail," he called loudly to be heard in the kitchen, "the food is cold. Bring me more meat fresh from the roasting. Bring thou also a very large portion for Tarkad, the son of my old friend, who is hungry and shall eat with me."

So ended the tale of Dabasir the camel trader of old Babylon. He found his own soul when he realized a great truth, a truth that had been known and used by wise men long before his time.

It has led men of all ages out of difficulties and into success and it will continue to do so for those who have the wisdom to understand its magic power. It is for any man to use who reads these lines.

9. The Clay Tablets From Babylon

Tablet I

Now, when the moon becometh full, I, Dabasir, who am but recently returned from slavery in Syria, with the determination to pay my many just debts and become a man of means worthy of respect in my native city of Babylon, do here engrave upon the clay a permanent record of my affairs to guide and assist me in carrying through my high desires.

Under the wise advice of my good friend Mathon, the gold lender, I am determined to follow an exact plan that he doth say will lead any honorable man out of debt into means and self-respect.

This plan includeth three purposes which are my hope and desire.

First, the plan doth provide for my future prosperity.

Therefore one-tenth of all I earn shall be set aside as my own to keep. For Mathon speaketh wisely when he saith:

"That man who keepeth in his purse both gold and silver that he need not spend is good to his family and loyal to his king.

"The man who hath but a few coppers in his purse is indifferent to his family and indifferent to his king.

"But the man who hath naught in his purse is unkind to his family and is disloyal to his king, for his own heart is bitter.

"Therefore, the man who wisheth to achieve must have coin that he may keep to jingle in his purse, that he have in his heart love for his family and loyalty to his king."

Second, the plan doth provide that I shall support and clothe my good wife who hath returned to me with loyalty from the house of her father. For Mathon doth say that to take good care of a faithful wife putteth self-respect into the heart of a man and addeth strength and determination to his purposes.

Therefore seven-tenths of all I earn shall be used to provide a home, clothes to wear, and food to eat, with a bit extra to spend, that our lives be not lacking in pleasure and enjoyment. But he doth further enjoin the greatest care that we spend not greater than seven-tenths of what I earn for these worthy purposes. Herein lieth the success of the plan. I must live upon this portion and never use more nor buy what I may not pay for out of this portion.

Tablet II

Third, the plan doth provide that out of my earnings my debts shall be paid.

Therefore each time the moon is full, two-tenths of all I have earned shall be divided honorably and fairly among those who have trusted me and to whom I am indebted. Thus in due time will all my indebtedness be surely paid.

Therefore, do I here engrave the name of every man to whom I am indebted and the honest amount of my debt.

Fahru, the cloth weaver, 2 silver, 6 copper.

Sinjar, the couch maker, 1 silver.

Ahmar, my friend, 3 silver, 1 copper.

Zankar, my friend, 4 silver, 7 copper,

Askamir, my friend, 1 silver, 3 copper.

Harinsir, the jewelmaker, 6 silver, 2 copper.

Diarbeker, my father's friend, 4 silver, 1 copper.

Alkahad, the house owner, 14 silver.

Mathon, the gold lender, 9 silver.

Birejik, the farmer, 1 silver, 7 copper.

(From here on, disintegrated. Cannot be deciphered.)

Tablet III

To these creditors do I owe in total one hundred and nineteen pieces of silver and one hundred and forty-one pieces of copper. Because I did owe these sums and saw no way to repay, in my folly I did permit my wife to return to her father and didst leave my native city and seek easy wealth elsewhere, only to find disaster and to see myself sold into the degradation of slavery.

Now that Mathon doth show me how I can repay my debts in small sums of my earnings, do I realize the great extent of my folly in running away from the results of my extravagances.

Therefore have I visited my creditors and explained to them that I have no resources with which to pay except my ability to earn, and that I intent to apply two-tenths of all I earn upon my indebtedness evenly and honestly. This much can I pay but no more. Therefore if they be patient, in time my obligations will be paid in full.

Ahmar, whom I thought my best friend, reviled me bitterly and I left him in humiliation. Birejik, the farmer, pleaded that I pay him first as he didst badly need help. Alkahad, the house owner, was indeed disagreeable and insisted that he would make me trouble unless I didst soon settle in full with him.

All the rest willingly accepted my proposal. Therefore am I more determined than ever to carry through, being convinced that it is easier to pay one's just debts than to avoid them. Even though I cannot meet the needs and demands of a few of my creditors I will deal impartially with all.

Tablet IV

Again the moon shines full. I have worked hard with a free mind. My good wife hath supported my intentions to pay my creditors. Because of our wise determination, I have earned during the past moon, buying camels of sound wind and good legs, for Nebatur, the sum of nineteen pieces of silver.

This I have divided according to the plan. One-tenth have I set aside to keep as my own, seven-tenths have I divided with my good wife to pay for our living. Two-tenths have I divided among my creditors as evenly as could be done in coppers.

I did not see Ahmar but left it with his wife. Birejik was so pleased he would kiss my hand. Old Alkahad alone was grouchy and said I must pay faster. To which I replied that if I were permitted to be well fed and not worried, that alone would enable me to pay faster. All the others thanked me and spoke well of my efforts.

Therefore, at the end of one moon, my indebtedness is reduced by almost four pieces of silver and I possess almost two pieces of silver besides, upon which no man hath claim. My heart is lighter than it hath been for a long time.

Again the moon shines full. I have worked hard but with poor success. Few camels have I been able to buy. Only eleven pieces of silver have I earned. Nevertheless my good wife and I have stood by the plan even though we have bought no new raiment and eaten little but herbs. Again I paid ourselves one-tenth of the eleven pieces, while we lived upon seven-tenths. I was surprised when Ahmar commended my payment, even though small. So did Birejik. Alkahad flew into a rage but when told to give back his portion if he did not wish it, he became reconciled. The others, as before, were content.

Again the moon shines full and I am greatly rejoiced. I intercepted a fine herd of camels and bought many sound ones, therefore my earnings were forty-two pieces of silver. This moon my wife and myself have bought much needed sandals and raiment. Also we have dined well on meat and fowl.

More than eight pieces of silver we have paid to our creditors. Even Alkahad did not protest.

Great is the plan for it leadeth us out of debt and giveth us wealth which is ours to keep.

Three times the moon had been full since I last carved upon this clay. Each time I paid to myself one-tenth of all I earned. Each time my good wife and I have lived upon seven-tenths even though at times it was difficult. Each time have I paid to my creditors two-tenths.

In my purse I now have twenty one pieces of silver that are mine. It maketh my head to stand straight upon my shoulders and maketh me proud to walk among my friends.

My wife keepeth well our home and is becomingly gowned. We are happy to live together.

The plan is of untold value. Hath it not made an honorable man of an ex-slave?

Tablet V

Again the moon shines full and I remember that it is long since I carved upon the clay. Twelve moons in truth have come and gone. But this day I will not neglect my record because upon this day I have paid the last of my debts. This is the day upon which my good wife and my thankful self celebrate with great feasting that our determination hath been achieved.

Many things occurred upon my final visit to my creditors that I shall long remember. Ahmar begged my forgiveness for his unkind words and said that I was one of all others he most desired for a friend.

Old Alkahad is not so bad after all, for he said, "Thou wert once a piece of soft clay to be pressed and molded by any hand that touched thee, but now thou art a piece of bronze capable of holding an edge. If thou needst silver or gold at any time come to me."

Nor is he the only one who holdeth me in high regard. Many others speak deferentially to me. My good wife looketh upon me with a light in her eyes that doth make a man have confidence in himself.

Yet it is the plan that hath made my success. It hath enabled me to pay all my debts and to jingle both gold and silver in my purse. I do commend it to all who wish to get ahead. For truly if it will enable an ex-slave to pay his debts and have gold in his purse, will it not aid any man to find independence? Nor am I, myself, finished with it, for I am convinced that if I follow it further it will make me rich among men.

10. The Luckiest Man in Babylon

At the head of his caravan, proudly rode Sharru Nada, the merchant prince of Babylon. He liked fine cloth and wore rich and becoming robes. He liked fine animals and sat easily upon his spirited Arabian stallion. To look at him one would hardly have guessed his advanced years. Certainly they would not have suspected that he was inwardly troubled.

The journey from Damascus is long and the hardships of the desert many. These he minded not. The Arab tribes are fierce and eager to loot rich caravans. These he feared not for his many fleet mounted guards were a safe protection.

About the youth at his side, whom he was bringing from Damascus, was he disturbed. This was Hadan Gula, the grandson of his partner of other years, Arad Gula, to whom he felt he owed a debt of gratitude which could never be repaid. He would like to do something for this grandson, but the more he considered this, the more difficult it seemed because of the youth himself.

Eyeing the young man's rings and earrings, he thought to himself, "He thinks jewels are for men, still he has his grandfather's strong face. But his grandfather wore no such gaudy robes. Yet, I sought him to come, hoping I might help him get a start for himself and get away from the wreck his father has made of their inheritance."

Hadan Gula broke in upon his thoughts, "Why dost thou work so hard, riding always with thy caravan upon its long journeys? Dost thou never take time to enjoy life?"

Sharru Nada smiled. "To enjoy life?" he repeated. "What wouldst thou do to enjoy life if thou wert Sharru Nada?"

"If I had wealth equal to thine, I would live like a prince. Never across the hot desert would I ride. I would spend the shekels as fast as they came to my purse. I would wear the richest of robes and the rarest of jewels. That would be a life to my liking, a life worth living." Both men laughed.

"Thy grandfather wore no jewels," Sharru Nada spoke before he thought, then continued jokingly, "Wouldst thou leave no time for work?"

"Work was made for slaves," Hadan Gula responded.

Sharra Nada bit his lip but made no reply, riding in silence until the trail led them to the slope. Here he reined his mount and pointing to the green valley far away, "See, there is the valley. Look far down and thou canst faintly see the walls of Babylon. The tower is the Temple of Bel. If thine eyes are sharp thou mayest even see the smoke from the eternal fire upon its crest."

"So that is Babylon? Always have I longed to see the wealthiest city in all the world," Hadan Gula commented. "Babylon, where my grandfather started his fortune. Would he were still alive. We would not be so sorely pressed."

"Why wish his spirit to linger on earth beyond its allotted time? Thou and thy father can well carry on his good work."

"Alas, of us, neither has his gift. Father and myself know not his secret for attracting the golden shekels."

Sharru Nada did not reply but gave rein to his mount and rode thoughtfully down the trail to the valley. Behind them followed the caravan in a cloud of reddish dust. Sometime later they reached the kings' highway and turned south through the irrigated farms.

Three old men plowing a field caught Sharru Nada's attention. They seemed strangely familiar. How ridiculous! One does not pass a field after forty years and find the same men plowing there. Yet, something within him said they were the same. One, with an uncertain grip, held the plow. The others laboriously plodded beside the oxen, ineffectually beating them with their barrel staves to keep them pulling.

Forty years ago he had envied these men! How gladly he would have exchanged places! But what a difference now. With pride he looked back at his trailing caravan, well-chosen camels and donkeys, loaded high with valuable goods from Damascus. All this was but one of his possessions.

He pointed to the plowers, saying, "Still plowing the same field where they were forty years ago."

"They look it, but why thinkest thou they are the same?"

"I saw them there," Sharru Nada replied.

Recollections were racing rapidly through his mind. Why could he not bury the past and live in the present? Then he saw, as in a picture, the smiling face of Arad Gula. The barrier between himself and the cynical youth beside him dissolved.

But how could he help such a superior youth with his spendthrift ideas and bejeweled hands? Work he could offer in plenty to willing workers, but naught for men who considered themselves too good for work. Yet he owed it to Arad Gula to do something, not a half-hearted attempt. He and Arad Gula had never done things that way. They were not that sort of men.

A plan came almost in a flash. There were objections. He must consider his own family and his own standing. It would be cruel; it would hurt. Being a man of quick decisions, he waived objections and decided to act.

"Wouldst thou be interested in hearing how thy worthy grandfather and myself joined in the partnership which proved so profitable?" he questioned.

“Why not just tell me how thou madest the golden shekels? That is all I need to know,” the young man parried.

Sharru Nada ignored the reply and continued, “We start with those men plowing. I was no older than thou. As the column of men in which I marched approached, good old Megiddo, the farmer, scoffed at the slip-shod way in which they plowed. Megiddo was chained next to me. ‘Look at the lazy fellows,’ he protested, ‘the plow holder makes no effort to plow deep, nor do the beaters keep the oxen in the furrow. How can they expect to raise a good crop with poor plowing?”

“Didst thou say Megiddo was chained to thee?” Hadan Gula asked in surprise.

“Yes, with bronze collars about our necks and a length of heavy chain between us. Next to him was Zabado, the sheep thief. I had known him in Harroun. At the end was a man we called Pirate because he told us not his name. We judged him as a sailor as he had entwined serpents tattooed upon his chest in sailor fashion. The column was made up thus so the men could walk in fours.”

“Thou wert chained as a slave?” Hadan Gula asked incredulously.

“Did not thy grandfather tell thee I was once a slave?”

“He often spoke of thee but never hinted of this.”

“He was a man thou couldst trust with innermost secrets. Thou, too, are a man I may trust, am I not right?” Sharru Nada looked him squarely in the eye.

“Thou mayest rely upon my silence, but I am amazed. Tell me how didst thou come to be a slave?”

Sharru Nada shrugged his shoulders, “Any man may find himself a slave. It was a gaming house and barley beer that brought me disaster. I was the victim of my brother’s indiscretions. In a brawl he killed his friend. I was bonded to the widow by my father, desperate to keep my brother from being prosecuted under the law. When my father could not raise the silver to free me, she in anger sold me to the slave dealer.”

“What a shame and injustice!” Hadan Gula protested. “But tell me, how didst thou regain freedom?”

“We shall come to that, but not yet. Let us continue my tale. As we passed, the plowers jeered at us. One did doff his ragged hat and bow low, calling out, ‘Welcome to Babylon, guests of the King. He waits for thee on the city walls where the banquet is spread, mud bricks and onion soup.’ With that they laughed uproariously.

“Pirate flew into a rage and cursed them roundly. ‘What do those men mean by the King awaiting us on the walls?' I asked him.

" 'To the city walls ye march to carry bricks until the back breaks. Maybe they beat thee to death before it breaks. They won't beat me. I'll kill 'em.'

"Then Megiddo spoke up, 'It doesn't make sense to me to talk of masters beating willing, hard-working slaves to death. Masters like good slaves and treat them well.'

" 'Who wants to work hard?' commented Zabado. 'Those plowers are wise fellows. They're not breaking their backs. Just letting on as if they be.'

" 'Thou can't get ahead by shirking,' Megiddo protested. 'If thou plow a hectare, that's a good day's work and any master knows it. But when thou plow only a half, that's shirking. I don't shirk. I like to work and I like to do good work, for work is the best friend I've ever known. It has brought me all the good things I've had, my farm and cows and crops, everything.'

" 'Yea, and where be these things, now?' scoffed Zabado. 'I figure it pays better to be smart and get by without working. You watch Zabado, if we're sold to the walls, he'll be carrying the water bag or some easy job when thou, who like to work, will be breaking thy back carrying bricks.' He laughed his silly laugh.

"Terror gripped me that night. I could not sleep. I crowded close to the guard rope, and when the others slept, I attracted the attention of Godoso who was doing the first guard watch. He was one of those brigand Arabs, the sort of rogue who, if he robbed thee of thy purse, would think he must also cut thy throat.

" 'Tell me, Godoso,' I whispered, 'when we get to Babylon will we be sold to the walls?'

" 'Why want to know?' he questioned cautiously.

" 'Canst thou not understand?' I pleaded. 'I am young. I want to live. I don't want to be worked or beaten to death on the walls. Is there any chance for me to get a good master?'

"He whispered back, 'I tell something. Thou good fellow, give Godoso no trouble. Most times we go first to slave market. Listen now. When buyers come, tell 'em you good worker, like to work hard for good master. Make 'em want to buy. You not make 'em buy, next day you carry brick. Mighty hard work.'

"After he walked away, I lay in the warm sand, looking up at the stars and thinking about work. What Megiddo had said about it being his best friend made me wonder if it would be my best friend. Certainly it would be if it helped me out of this.

"When Megiddo awoke, I whispered my good news to him. It was our one ray of hope as we marched toward Babylon. Late in the afternoon we approached the walls and could see the lines of men, like black ants, climbing up and down the steep diagonal paths. As we drew closer, we were amazed at the thousands of men working; some were digging in the moat, others mixed the dirt into mud bricks. The greatest numbers were carrying the bricks in large baskets up those steep trails to the masons.*

"Overseers cursed the laggards and cracked bullock whips over the backs of those who failed to keep in line. Poor, worn-out fellows were seen to stagger and fall beneath their heavy baskets, unable to rise again. If the lash failed to bring them to their feet, they were pushed to the side of the paths and left writhing in agony. Soon they would be dragged down to join other craven bodies beside the roadway to await un-sanctified graves. As I beheld the ghastly sight, I shuddered. So this was what awaited my father's son if he failed at the slave market.

"Godoso had been right. We were taken through the gates of the city to the slave prison and next morning marched to the pens in the market. Here the rest of the men huddled in fear and only the whips of our guard could keep them moving so the buyers could examine them. Megiddo and myself eagerly talked to every man who permitted us to address him.

"The slave dealer brought soldiers from the king's guard who shackled Pirate and brutally beat him when he protested. As they led him away, I felt sorry for him.

"Megiddo felt that we would soon part. When no buyers were near, he talked to me earnestly to impress upon me how valuable work would be to me in the future: 'Some men hate it. They make it their enemy. Better to treat it like a friend, make thyself like it. Don't mind because it is hard. If thou thinkest about what a good house thou build, then who cares if the beams are heavy and it is far from the well to carry the water for the plaster. Promise me, boy, if thou get a master, work for him as hard as thou canst. If he does not appreciate all thou do, never mind. Remember, work, well-done, does good to the man who does it. It makes him a better man.' He stopped as a burly farmer came to the enclosure and looked at us critically.

"Megiddo asked about his farm and crops, soon convincing him that he would be a valuable man. After violent bargaining with the slave dealer, the farmer drew a fat purse from beneath his robe, and soon Megiddo had followed his new master out of sight.

"A few other men were sold during the morning. At noon Godoso confided to me that the dealer was disgusted and would not stay over another night but would take all who remained at sundown to the king's buyer. I was becoming desperate when a fat, good-natured man walked up to the wall and inquired if there was a baker among us.

"I approached him saying, 'Why should a good baker like thyself seek another baker of inferior ways? Would it not be easier to teach a willing man like myself thy skilled ways? Look at me, I am young, strong and like to work. Give me a chance and I will do my best to earn gold and silver for thy purse.'

* The works of Babylon, its walls, temples, hanging gardens and great canals, were built by slave labor, mainly prisoners of war. This slave workforce also included many citizens of Babylon and its provinces who had been sold into slavery because of crimes or financial troubles. It was a common custom for men to put themselves, their wives or their children up as bond to guarantee payment. In case of default, those bonded were sold into slavery.

"He was impressed by my willingness and began bargaining with the dealer who had never noticed me since he had bought me but now waxed eloquent on my abilities, good health and good disposition. I felt like a fat ox being sold to a butcher. At last, much to my joy, the deal was closed. I followed my new master away, thinking I was the luckiest man in Babylon.

"My new home was much to my liking. Nana-naid, my master, taught me how to grind the barley in the stone bowl that stood in the courtyard, how to build the fire in the oven and then how to grind very fine the sesame flour for the honey cakes. I had a couch in the shed where his grain was stored. The old slave housekeeper, Swasti, fed me well and was pleased at the way I helped her with the heavy tasks.

"Here was the chance I had longed for to make myself valuable to my master and, I hoped, to find a way to earn my freedom.

"I asked Nana-naid to show me how to knead the bread and to bake. This he did, much pleased at my willingness. Later, when I could do this well, I asked him to show me how to make the honey cakes, and soon I was doing all the baking. My master was glad to be idle, but Swasti shook her head in disapproval, 'No work to do is bad for any man,' she declared.

"I felt it was time for me to think of a way by which I might start to earn coins to buy my freedom. As the baking was finished at noon, I thought Nana-naid would approve if I found profitable employment for the afternoons and might share my earnings with me. Then the thought came to me, why not bake more of the honey cakes and peddle them to hungry men upon the streets of the city?

"I presented my plan to Nana-naid this way: 'If I can use my afternoons after the baking is finished to earn for thee coins, would it be only fair for thee to share my earnings with me that I might have money of my own to spend for those things which every man desires and needs?'

" 'Fair enough, fair enough,' he admitted. When I told him of my plan to peddle our honey cakes, he was well pleased. 'Here is what we will do,' he suggested. 'Thou sellest them at two for a penny, then half of the pennies will be mine to pay for the flour and the honey and the wood to bake them. Of the rest, I shall take half and thou shall keep half.'

"I was much pleased by his generous offer that I might keep for myself, one-fourth of my sales. That night I worked late to make a tray upon which to display them. Nana-naid gave me one of his worn robes that I might look well, and Swasti helped me patch it and wash it clean.

"The next day I baked an extra supply of honey cakes. They looked brown and tempting upon the tray as I went along the street, loudly calling my wares. At first no one seemed interested, and I became discouraged. I kept on and later in the afternoon as men became hungry, the cakes began to sell and soon my tray was empty.

"Nana-naid was well pleased with my success and gladly paid me my share. I was delighted to own pennies. Megiddo had been right when he said a master appreciated good work from his slaves. That night I was so excited over my success I could hardly sleep and tried to figure how much I could earn in a year and how many years would be required to buy my freedom.

"As I went forth with my tray of cakes every day, I soon found regular customers. One of these was none other than thy grandfather, Arad Gula. He was a rug merchant and sold to the housewives, going from one end of the city to the other, accompanied by a donkey loaded high with rugs and a black slave to tend it. He would buy two cakes for himself and two for his slave, always tarrying to talk with me while they ate them.

"Thy grandfather said something to me one day that I shall always remember. 'I like thy cakes, boy, but better still I like the fine enterprise with which thou offerest them. Such spirit can carry thee far on the road to success.'

"But how canst thou understand, Hadan Gula, what such words of encouragement could mean to a slave boy, lonesome in a great city, struggling with all he had in him to find a way out of his humiliation?

"As the months went by I continued to add pennies to my purse. It began to have a comforting weight upon my belt. Work was proving to be my best friend just as Megiddo had said. I was happy but Swasti was worried.

" 'Thy master, I fear to have him spend so much time at the gaming houses,' she protested.

"I was overjoyed one day to meet my friend Megiddo upon the street. He was leading three donkeys loaded with vegetables to the market. 'I am doing mighty well,' he said. 'My master does appreciate my good work for now I am a foreman. See, he does trust the marketing to me, and also he is sending for my family. Work is helping me to recover from my great trouble. Someday it will help me to buy my freedom and once more own a farm of my own.'

"Time went on and Nana-naid became more and more anxious for me to return from selling. He would be waiting when I returned and would eagerly count and divide our money. He would also urge me to seek further markets and increase my sales.

"Often I went outside the city gates to solicit the overseers of the slaves building the walls. I hated to return to the disagreeable sights but found the overseers liberal buyers. One day I was surprised to see Zabado waiting in line to fill his basket with bricks. He was gaunt and bent, and his back was covered with welts and sores from the whips of the overseers. I was sorry for him and handed him a cake which he crushed into his mouth like a hungry animal. Seeing the greedy look in his eyes, I ran before he could grab my tray.

" 'Why dost thou work so hard?' Arad Gula said to me one day. Almost the same question thou asked of me today, dost thou remember? I told him what Megiddo had said about work and how it was proving to be my best friend. I showed him with pride my wallet of pennies and explained how I was saving them to buy my freedom.

" 'When thou art free, what wilt thou do?' he inquired.

" 'Then,' I answered, 'I intend to become a merchant.'

"At that, he confided in me. Something I had never suspected. 'Thou knowest not that I, also, am a slave. I am in partnership with my master.'"

"Stop," demanded Hadan Gula. 'I will not listen to lies defaming my grandfather. He was no slave." His eyes blazed in anger.

Sharru Nada remained calm. "I honor him for rising above his misfortune and becoming a leading citizen of Damascus. Art thou, his grandson, cast of the same mold? Art thou man enough to face true facts, or dost thou prefer to live under false illusions?"

Hadan Gula straightened in his saddle. In a voice suppressed with deep emotion he replied, "My grandfather was beloved by all. Countless were his good deeds. When the famine came did not his gold buy grain in Egypt and did not his caravan bring it to Damascus and distribute it to the people so none would starve? Now thou sayest he was but a despised slave in Babylon."

"Had he remained a slave in Babylon, then he might well have been despised, but when, through his own efforts, he became a great man in Damascus, the gods indeed condoned his misfortunes and honored him with their respect," Sharru Nada replied.

"After telling me that he was a slave," Sharru Nada continued, 'he explained how anxious he had been to earn his freedom. Now that he had enough money to buy this he was much disturbed as to what he should do. He was no longer making good sales and feared to leave the support of his master.

"I protested his indecision: 'Cling no longer to thy master. Get once again the feeling of being a free man. Act like a free man and succeed like one! Decide what thou desirest to accomplish and then work will aid thee to achieve it!' He went on his way saying he was glad I had shamed him for his cowardice.**

"One day I went outside the gates again, and was surprised to find a great crowd gathering there. When I asked a man for an explanation he replied: "Hast thou not heard? An escaped slave who murdered one of the king's guards has been brought to justice and will this day be flogged to death for his crime. Even the king himself is to be here.'

"So dense was the crowd about the flogging post, I feared to go near lest my tray of honey cakes be upset. Therefore, I climbed up the unfinished wall to see over the heads of the people. I was fortunate in having a view of Nebuchadnezzar himself as he rode by in his golden chariot. Never had I beheld such grandeur, such robes and hangings of gold cloth and velvet.

"I could not see the flogging though I could hear the shrieks of the poor slave. I wandered how one so noble as our handsome king could endure to see such suffering, yet when I saw he was laughing and joking with his nobles, I knew he was cruel and understood why such inhuman tasks were demanded of the slaves building the walls.

"After the slave was dead, his body was hung upon a pole by a rope attached to his leg so all might see. As the crowd began to thin, I went close. On the hairy chest, I saw tattooed, two entwined serpents. It was Pirate.

"The next time I met Arad Gula he was a changed man. Full of enthusiasm he greeted me: 'Behold, the slave thou knewest is now a free man. There was magic in thy words. Already my sales and my profits my master. She much desires that we move to a strange city where no man shall know I was once a slave. Thus our children shall be above reproach for their father's misfortune. Work has become my best helper. It has enabled me to recapture my confidence and my skill to sell.'

"I was overjoyed that I had been able, even in a small way, to repay him for the encouragement he had given me.

** Slave customs in Babylon, though they seem inconsistent to us, were strictly regulated by law. For example, a slave could own property, even other slaves upon which his master had no claim. Slaves intermarried freely with non-slaves. Children of free mothers were free. Most of the city merchants were slaves, many were in partnership with their masters and wealthy in their own right.

"One evening Swasti came to me in deep distress: 'Thy master is in trouble. I fear for him. Some months ago he lost much at the gaming tables. He pays not the farmer for his grain nor his honey. He pays not the money lender. They are angry and threaten him.'

" 'Why should we worry over his folly. We are not his keepers,' I replied thoughtlessly.

" 'Foolish youth, thou understandeth not. To the money lender didst he give thy title to secure a loan. Under the law he can claim thee and sell thee. I know not what to do. He is a good master. Why? Oh why, should such trouble come upon him?'

"Not were Swasti's fears groundless. While I was doing the baking next morning, the money lender returned with a man he called Sasi. This man looked me over and said I would do.

"The money lender waited not for my master to return but told Swasti to tell him he had taken me. With only the robe on my back and the purse of pennies hanging safely from my belt, I was hurried away from the unfinished baking.

"I was whirled away from my dearest hopes as the hurricane snatches the tree from the forest and casts it into the surging sea. Again a gaming house and barley beer had caused me disaster.

"Sasi was a blunt, gruff man. As he led me across the city, I told him of the good work I had been doing for Nana-naid and said I hoped to do good work for him. His reply offered no encouragement:

" 'I like not this work. My master likes it not. The king has told him to send me to build a section of the Grand Canal. Master tells Sasi to buy more slaves, work hard and finish quick. Bah, how can any man finish a big job quick?'

"Picture a desert with not a tree, just low shrubs and a sun burning with such fury the water in our barrels became so hot we could scarcely drink it. Then picture rows of men, going down into the deep excavation and lugging heavy baskets of dirt up soft, dusty trails from daylight until dark. Picture food served in open troughs from which we helped ourselves like swine. We had no tents, no straw for beds. That was the situation in which I found myself. I buried my wallet in a marked spot, wondering if I would ever dig it up again.

"At first I worked with good will, but as the months dragged on, I felt my spirit breaking. Then the heat fever took hold of my weary body. I lost my appetite and could scarcely eat the mutton and vegetables. At night I would toss in unhappy wakefulness.

"In my misery, I wondered if Zabado had not the best plan, to shirk and keep his back from being broken in work. Then I recalled my last sight of him and knew his plan was not good.

"I thought of Pirate with his bitterness and wondered if it might be just as well to fight and kill. The memory of his bleeding body reminded me that his plan was also useless.

"Then I remembered my last sight of Megiddo. His hands were deeply calloused from hard work but his heart was light and there was happiness on his face. His was the best plan.

"Yet I was just as willing to work as Megiddo; he could not have worked harder than I. Why did not my work bring me happiness and success? Was it work that brought Megiddo happiness, or was happiness and success merely in the laps of the Gods? Was I to work the rest of my life without gaining my desires, without happiness and success? All of these questions were jumbled in my mind and I had not an answer. Indeed, I was sorely confused.

"Several days later when it seemed that I was at the end of my endurance and my questions still unanswered, Sasi sent for me. A messenger had come from my master to take me back to Babylon. I dug up my precious wallet, wrapped myself in the tattered remnants of my robe and was on my way.

"As we rode, the same thoughts of a hurricane whirling me hither and thither kept racing through my feverish brain. I seemed to be living the weird words of a chant from my native town of Harroun:

Besetting a man like a whirlwind,
Driving him like a storm,
Whose course no one can foliate,
Whose destiny no one can foretell.

"Was I destined to be ever thus punished for I knew not what? What new miseries and disappointments awaited me?

"When we rode to the courtyard of my master's house, imagine my surprise when I saw Arad Gula awaiting me. He helped me down and hugged me like a long lost brother.

"As we went our way I would have followed him as a slave should follow his master, but he would not permit me. He put his arm about me, saying, 'I hunted everywhere for thee. When I had almost given up hope, I did meet Swasti who told me of the money lender, who directed me to thy noble owner. A hard bargain he did drive and made me pay an outrageous price, but thou art worth it. Thy philosophy and thy enterprise have been my inspiration to this new success.'

" 'Megiddo's philosophy, not mine,' I interrupted.

" 'Megiddo's and thine. Thanks to thee both, we are going to Damascus and I need thee for my partner. See,' he exclaimed, 'in one moment thou will be a free man!' So saying he drew from beneath his robe the clay tablet carrying my title. This he raised above his head and hurled it to break in a hundred pieces upon the cobblestones. With glee he stamped upon the fragments until they were but dust.

"Tears of gratitude filled my eyes. I knew I was the luckiest man in Babylon.

"Work, thou see, by this, in the time of my greatest distress, didst prove to be my best friend. My willingness to work enabled me to escape from being sold to join the slave gangs upon the walls. It also so impressed thy grandfather, he selected me for his partner."

Then Hadan Gula questioned, "Was work my grandfather's secret key to the golden shekels?"

"It was the only key he had when I first knew him," Sharru Nada replied. "Thy grandfather enjoyed working. The gods appreciated his efforts and rewarded him liberally."

"I begin to see," Hadan Gula was speaking thoughtfully. "Work attracted his many friends who admired his industry and the success it brought. Work brought him the honors he enjoyed so much in Damascus. Work brought him all those things I have approved. And I thought work was fit only for slaves."

"Life is rich with many pleasures for men to enjoy," Sharru Nada commented. "Each has its place. I am glad that work is not reserved for slaves. Were that the case I would be deprived of my greatest pleasure. Many things do I enjoy but nothing takes the place of work."

Sharru Nada and Hadan Gula rode in the shadows of the towering walls up to the massive, bronze gates of Babylon. At their approach the gate guards jumped to attention and respectfully saluted an honored citizen. With head held high Sharru Nada led the long caravan through the gates and up the streets of the city.

"I have always hoped to be a man like my grandfather," Hadan Gula confided to him. "Never before did I realize just what kind of man he was. This thou hast shown me. Now that I understand, I do admire him all the more and feel more determined to be like him. I fear I can never repay thee for giving me the true key to his success. From this day forth, I shall use his key. I shall start humbly as he started, which befits my true station far better than jewels and fine robes."

So saying Hadan Gula pulled the jeweled baubles from his ears and the rings from his fingers. Then reining his horse, he dropped back and rode with deep respect behind the leader of the caravan.

11. A Historical Sketch of Babylon

In the pages of history there lives no city more glamorous than Babylon. Its very name conjures visions of wealth and splendor. Its treasures of gold and jewels were fabulous. One naturally pictures such a wealthy city as located in a suitable setting of tropical luxury, surrounded by rich natural resources of forests, and mines. Such was not the case. It was located beside the Euphrates River, in a flat, arid valley. It had no forests, no mines—not even stone for building. It was not even located upon a natural trade-route. The rainfall was insufficient to raise crops.

Babylon is an outstanding example of man's ability to achieve great objectives, using whatever means are at his disposal. All of the resources supporting this large city were man-developed. All of its riches were man-made.

Babylon possessed just two natural resources—a fertile soil and water in the river. With one of the greatest engineering accomplishments of this or any other day, Babylonian engineers diverted the waters from the river by means of dams and immense irrigation canals. Far out across that arid valley went these canals to pour the life giving waters over the fertile soil. This ranks among the first engineering feats known to history. Such abundant crops as were the reward of this irrigation system the world had never seen before.

Fortunately, during its long existence, Babylon was ruled by successive lines of kings to whom conquest and plunder were but incidental. While it engaged in many wars, most of these were local or defensive against ambitious conquerors from other countries who coveted the fabulous treasures of Babylon. The outstanding rulers of Babylon live in history because of their wisdom, enterprise and justice. Babylon produced no strutting monarchs who sought to conquer the known world that all nations might pay homage to their egotism.

As a city, Babylon exists no more. Today, this valley of the Euphrates, once a populous irrigated farming district, is again a wind-swept arid waste. Gone are the fertile fields, the mammoth cities and the long caravans of rich merchandise.

Dotting this valley are earthen hills. For centuries, they were considered by travelers to be nothing else. The attention of archaeologists were finally attracted to them because of broken pieces of pottery and brick washed down by the occasional rain storms.

Many scientists consider the civilization of Babylon and other cities in this valley to be the oldest of which there is a definite record. Positive dates have been proved reaching back 8,000 years. An interesting fact in this connection is the means used to determine these dates. Uncovered in the ruins of Babylon were descriptions of an eclipse of the sun. Modern astronomers readily computed the time when such an eclipse, visible in Babylon, occurred and thus established a known relationship between their calendar and our own.

In this way, we have proved that 8,000 years ago, the Sumerites, who inhabited Babylonia, were living in walled cities. One can only conjecture for how many centuries previous such cities had existed. Their inhabitants were not mere barbarians living within protecting walls. They were an educated and enlightened people. So far as written history goes, they were the first engineers, the first astronomers, the first mathematicians, the first financiers and the first people to have a written language.

In addition to irrigating the valley lands, Babylonian engineers completed another project of similar magnitude. By means of an elaborate drainage system they reclaimed an immense area of swamp land at the mouths of the Euphrates and Tigris Rivers and put this also under cultivation.

Herodotus, the Greek traveler and historian, visited Babylon while it was in its prime and has given us the only known description by an outsider. His writings give a graphic description of the city and some of the unusual customs of its people. He mentions the remarkable fertility of the soil and the bountiful harvest of wheat and barley which they produced.

The glory of Babylon has faded but its wisdom has been preserved for us. For this we are indebted to their form of records. In that distant day, the use of paper had not been invented. Instead, they laboriously engraved their writing upon tablets of moist clay. When completed, these were baked and became hard tile. In size, they were about six by eight inches, and an inch in thickness.

These clay tablets, as they are commonly called, were used much as we use modern forms of writing. Upon them were engraved legends, poetry, history, transcriptions of royal decrees, the laws of the land, titles to property, promissory notes and even letters which were dispatched by messengers to distant cities. From these clay tablets we are permitted an insight into the intimate, personal affairs of the people.

One of the outstanding wonders of Babylon was the immense walls surrounding the city. The ancients ranked them with the great pyramid of Egypt as belonging to the "seven wonders of the world." Queen Semiramis is credited with having erected the first walls during the early history of the city. Modern excavators have been unable to find any trace of the original walls. Nor is their exact height known. From mention made by early writers, it is estimated they were about fifty to sixty feet high, faced on the outer side with burnt brick and further protected by a deep moat of water.

The later and more famous walls were started about six hundred years before the time of Christ by King Nabopolassar. Upon such a gigantic scale did he plan the rebuilding, he did not live to see the work finished. This was left to his son, Nebuchadnezzar, whose name is familiar in Biblical history.

The height and length of these later walls staggers belief. They are reported upon reliable authority to have been about one hundred and sixty feet high, the equivalent of the height of a modern fifteen story office building. The total length is estimated as between nine and eleven miles. So wide was the top that a six horse chariot could be driven around them.

The city of Babylon was organized much like a modern city. There were streets and shops. Peddlers offered their wares through residential districts. Priests officiated in magnificent temples. Within the city was an inner enclosure for the royal palaces. The walls about this were said to have been higher than those about the city.

The Babylonians were skilled in the arts. These included sculpture, painting, weaving, gold working and the manufacture of metal weapons and agricultural implements. Their jewelers created most artistic jewelry. Many samples have been recovered from the graves of its wealthy citizens and are now on exhibition in the leading museums of the world.

At a very early period when the rest of the world was still hacking at trees with stone-headed axes, or hunting and fighting with flint-pointed spears and arrows, the Babylonians were using axes, spears and arrows with metal heads.

The Babylonians were clever financiers and traders. So far as we know, they were the original inventors of money as a means of exchange, of promissory notes and written titles to property.

Babylon was never entered by hostile armies until about 540 years before the birth of Christ. Even then the walls were not captured. The story of the fall of Babylon is most unusual. Cyrus, one of the great conquerors of that period, intended to attack the city and hoped to take its impregnable walls. Advisors of Nabonidus, the King of Babylon, persuaded him to go forth to meet Cyrus and give him battle without waiting for the city to be besieged. In the succeeding defeat to the Babylonian army, it fled away from the city. Cyrus, thereupon, entered the open gates and took possession without resistance.

The eons of time have crumbled to dust the proud walls of its temples, but the wisdom of Babylon endures.